Sunset

Ideas for
Kitchen
Storage

Ideas & Projects

By the Editors
of Sunset Books
and
Sunset Magazine

LANE PUBLISHING CO. ● Menlo Park, California

We thank . . .

. . . the many architects, designers, and homeowners whose ideas have come together in this book. A special acknowledgment is due Allmilmö Cabinets by Plus Kitchens, and Dada North American, Inc. To Kathryn L. Arthurs and Hilary Hannon go our thanks for their work in assembling the color section.

Sunset Books
   Editor, David E. Clark
   Managing Editor, Elizabeth L. Hogan

Sixth printing February 1988

Cover: Open Shelves, Hang-ups, and Built-ins

Cooking utensils, measuring cups, and mixer attachments queue up along a strip of stainless steel hooks (made by a fabricator of store display racks). Handsome beech counter below features a built-in unit to power a number of attachments, including this juicer. Open shelves above hold stacks of dishes and a set of custom-made acrylic canisters; tabs on canisters pull to dispense staples. Architect: David Stovell. Photographed by Nikolay Zurek. Cover design by Zan Fox.

Book Editors:

Maureen Williams Zimmerman
Helen Sweetland

Staff Researcher: **Donice G. Evans**

Contributing Editor: **Marian May**

Design: **Roger Flanagan**

Illustrations: **Joe Seney**

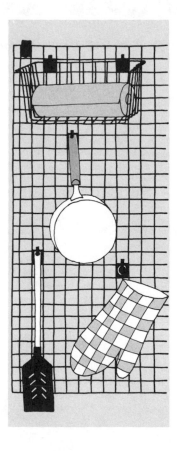

Contents

INTRODUCTION

Maximum use calls for maximum access

"I need more storage space!" is a familiar and frequent wail from the kitchen, usually as something new, like a food processor or casserole dish, is being crammed into an already bulging cupboard.

Generally, it's not just a matter of too little space. Somehow, you always make room—stacking, pushing aside, shoving into an inaccessible corner—with the result that the new utensil or appliance, or whatever it displaced, is rarely dug out and used.

Maximum use calls for maximum access. Since this principle is basic to serious kitchen storage planning, this book focuses on ideas for *active* storage, the placement of things you use regularly.

Guidelines for good storage

Whether you're trying to increase the storage in your kitchen in the simplest and least expensive way possible, or designing the ultimate in storage for a brand-new kitchen, these guidelines can help you through the project.

First, determine your needs and priorities. If you love to bake, you'll need more than average space for utensils, special baking pans, and perhaps a heavy-duty mixer. If your specialty is stir-fried dishes, you'll want a place for sharp knives (see pages 52–53), a wok, and a cutting board next to the cooktop. Whatever your interests, put yourself in the middle of your kitchen and mentally put away all the equipment you use most often; you'll then have an individualized storage plan that meets your needs.

The second step is to choose the right kind of storage for your needs. Though built-in cabinets (pages 8–15) and shelves (pages 32–39) carry the main burden of storage in most kitchens, you don't necessarily have to rip out the old cabinets and install new ones. Instead, consider the exciting variety of auxiliary storage units you see pictured throughout this book. Stacking bins are inexpensive, handy containers for cleaning equipment, produce, even toys. Handsome hooks and hang-

At the root of modern kitchen storage: the Hoosier cabinet

Many of our modern ideas about kitchen storage and food preparation centers aren't new at all; in fact, they can be traced back to those big, boxy cabinets that revolutionized American kitchens—the Hoosiers. Manufactured from the late 1800s until World War II, these hold-it-all cabinets were the first mass-produced, popular kitchen aids to combine a food preparation area and a multitude of storage compartments in one compact unit. Early ads for the Hoosier cabinets claimed that they reduced kitchen work by half—and many housewives would probably have agreed.

Every cubic inch of the Hoosier was put to good use. There were lots of drawers for spices, silverware, knives, and mixing spoons. Some models were also available with sugar and cornmeal bins, a tin-lined bread drawer, and a built-in flour bin and sifter—welcome luxuries in the days when the family bread supply was baked at home.

The two big doors in the base of the Hoosier opened to reveal pot storage on shelves only half the depth of the cabinet. This allowed ample room on the inside of the doors for racks of pot lids and cooky sheets, a convenience now being designed into many contemporary cabinets.

Overhead were cabinets, sometimes behind frosted glass, for china and crystal treasures. Everyday dishes were stacked conveniently in the wide opening that was often closed off with a roll-up tambour door.

Tying the Hoosier all together was a recessed porcelain-enameled work counter that was pulled out whenever extra table space was needed—at jelly-making time, at Thanksgiving for wrestling the turkey, or for afternoon lemonade and homework.

When modern kitchens with built-in cabinets became the rule instead of the exception, the Hoosier, having loaned out all its ideas for compact storage and work space, was relegated to the garage.

But the disappearance of the Hoosier cabinet was merely temporary. Today, these handsome almost-antiques are being incorporated into some contemporary kitchens. Look for them in antique stores—if you're not lucky enough to have one hidden away in your basement or garage.

ers can hold aprons and dishtowels, as well as pots and pans. And lazy Susans can bring to life the lost space in the back of a corner cabinet.

Finally, how do you obtain the units you've selected? At one extreme, this step can mean the considerable expense of having new built-in cabinetry custom created by a cabinetmaker; at the other, it involves no more than buying or building some simple hanging devices, racks, drawer organizers, or shelves. A quick walk through your local hardware store or kitchen cabinet showroom will turn up lots of ideas; a more concentrated survey of what's on the market can start with brochures from the major manufacturers (see pages 78–79).

Guidelines for maximum access

Following some simple guidelines will maximize space and accessibility in your kitchen, no matter what kind of storage structures you have.

• Store frequently used items between knee and eye level.

• Store items where you use them most. If you use an item in several locations, store it at the first or last place you use it (for example, dinnerware can be stored near the dinner table or next to the dishwasher). If it's an inexpensive item, consider buying several and storing one in each place you use it.

• Items used together should be stored together. It doesn't make any sense to keep your electric hand mixer in a wall cabinet on one side of the kitchen and the beaters in a drawer on the other side.

• Design cabinets and shelves to the cook's height and reach (keeping in mind that any substantial departure from the norm could be a factor if you decide to sell the house). In an existing kitchen that can't be adjusted, add a roll-around work table that's the right height; use a sturdy step stool to reach high wall cabinets.

• Don't stack items on top of one another. That way you won't have to move several items you don't need before you reach the one you do need.

• Arrange canned and packaged goods in a single row on a door rack or on shallow shelves. With single-row storage you won't have to shove cans aside to find the one you want.

• Use inexpensive storage aids such as door racks, turntables, drawer dividers, and roll-out shelves to customize existing cabinets.

• Review your storage situation from time to time. If you haven't used an item in ages, consider moving it out of the kitchen or giving it away. Reserve precious kitchen storage space for items you use regularly.

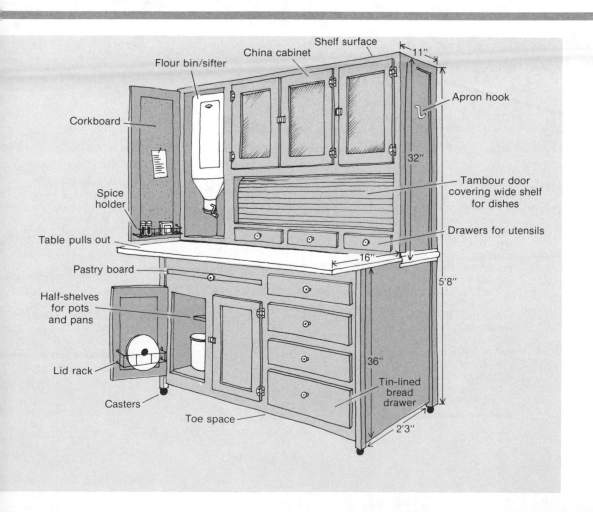

INTRODUCTION

Consider the tasks at hand

Imagine it's time to add the crucial ingredient to the dish you're cooking. You must keep stirring, but what you need is on the other side of the room. If you often find yourself doing unplanned reaching and stretching exercises in your kitchen, it may be time to rearrange your storage.

Most kitchen activities take place within the triangle formed by the three major kitchen appliances—the refrigerator, the range, and the sink. Think of each point

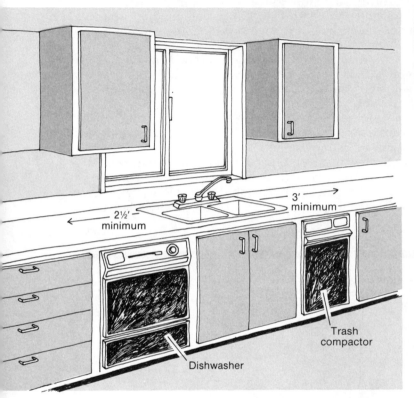

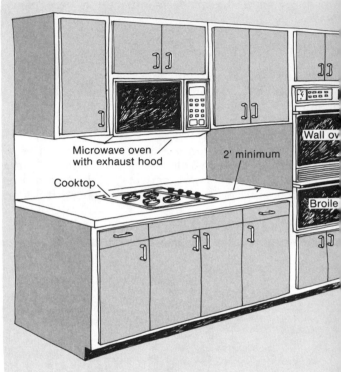

Sink Center

Besides the obvious—a sink—this center may include a dishwasher, garbage disposer, and trash compactor, as well as cabinets and drawers. In this area, food is rinsed and trimmed, wastes and recyclables are disposed of, dishes are washed and stored.

Provide storage space for chopping board, food preparation utensils, wastebasket, and dishwashing and cleaning supplies. Stow dishes and glassware as close as possible to dishwasher for easy unloading. Underneath sink is a convenient spot for storing paper bags.

Cooking Center

Range—or cooktop with separate oven—is focus of cooking center, which can also include a microwave or convection oven and several electric cooking appliances.

In base cabinets, store pots and pans, cooky sheets, roasting racks, and muffin tins. Fill drawers with spoons and spatulas and other cooking utensils. You'll also want to keep potholders and condiments within easy reach.

of the triangle as a separate and distinct center; then plan storage appropriate to each. If you have some extra space, include a food preparation center, as well.

Above all, keep an open mind when you're planning your work centers. If space is at a premium in your kitchen, combine some of the centers; but if space is not a problem, you may want to develop additional work centers—an office center, play center, dining center, or beverage center, for example—to fit your own needs.

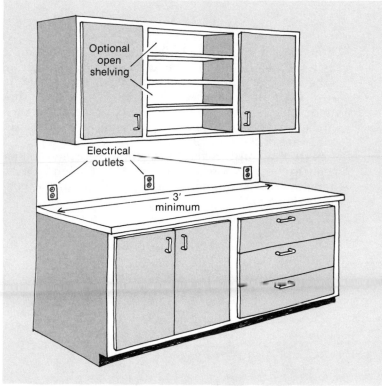

Refrigerator Center

Often, this center consists of not only a refrigerator and several cabinets, but also a floor-to-ceiling pantry or broom closet wedged between refrigerator and adjacent wall. If you store nonperishable food items near refrigerator, putting groceries away is a snap. Tuck plastic wrap, foil, plastic bags, and freezer containers in a nearby drawer or cabinet.

In hard-to-reach cabinet above refrigerator, keep extra rolls of paper towels or infrequently used items such as picnic supplies and party goods.

Preparation Center

If you have extra room in your kitchen, design a food preparation center with storage for small appliances—food processor, toaster, mixer, can opener, for example. Locating center near refrigerator and/or sink simplifies mixing and serving chores. Keep cook books and recipe boxes close by. With canisters, mixing bowls, and small utensils in cabinets and drawers, you'll waste little motion preparing meals.

CABINETS
Setting the storage style

More than anything else in the kitchen, cabinets set the style and determine how the room looks—ranging from a mellow spot where family and friends congregate, to a sophisticated European-style kitchen with a slick modern emphasis. Often, the total appearance of a kitchen can be suggested simply by the style, finish, or hardware of the cabinet doors.

Style must also relate to function, because cabinets need to be workhorses, able to conceal behind closed doors literally hundreds of items you'll want on hand in the kitchen.

If you're not planning to install new cabinets, you can update the looks of your old ones—and sometimes get more work out of them, too—simply by replacing or redecorating the cabinet doors or changing simple accessories such as door pulls.

• Remove old doors and drawer fronts; build new ones from lengths of ¾-inch oak or oak plywood panels.

• Attach a decorative grid of half-rounds. Or remove old moldings, then sand and repaint or restain the cabinets for an uncluttered look.

• Leaving the framework as is, paint the doors a fresh new color.

• Install sliding or push-up doors, especially convenient in overhead locations.

• When there's no room for a cabinet door, hang venetian blinds, canvas curtains that slide on rings along a wall-mounted dowel supported in midspan, or bamboo blinds.

• Round, smoothly sanded holes in the corner of a door are a substitute for door pulls. A decorative wood strip extending a bit below the bottom of each wall cabinet door also eliminates the need for pulls.

• Cover just the cabinet doors with wallpaper, or go all out and cover everything—walls, ceiling, even the refrigerator. (Covering an entire room with small-print wallpaper will make the room look larger.)

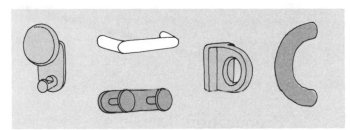

▲
DOUBLE-USE KNOBS

These cabinet knobs and handles can accommodate potholders and towels.

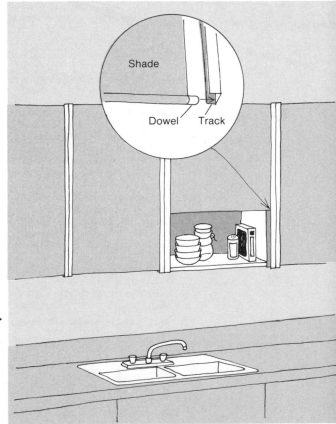

**SHADES ENCLOSE ▶
CABINETS**

Bright fabric, canvas, or heavy plastic shades replace cabinet doors. Dowels in bottom hems run in tracks along cabinet sides. Pulls can be added.

◄ BEFORE: DARK AND DULL WITH STANDARDIZED STORAGE

Small, drab kitchen is overwhelmed by heavy, dark cabinetry. In spite of window at left, room is dark and faintly oppressive. Wall and base cabinets have typical stationary shelves.

◄ AFTER: BRIGHT AND INVITING WITH SPECIALIZED STORAGE

Though no walls were moved, kitchen appears larger. Mirror replaces window, and newly symmetrical room has focal point: glass-doored display cabinet at end. Office at opposite end of kitchen is completely integrated into cabinet design and is better suited to owner's needs than additional food or utensil storage. Several base cabinets feature pull-out wire shelves. Architect: Gilbert Oliver.

CABINETS

Distinctive designs for a unique kitchen look

▲
OPEN TO VIEW: CHEERFUL RED CABINETS

Glossy, tomato-tone wall and base cabinets brighten a house that has generous expanses of white wall. Loft kitchen is open on one side to floors above and below.
Architect: Willard Martin of Martin/Soderstrom/Matteson.

Cabinets are the basic elements both in your kitchen storage scheme and your kitchen decor. If you have a new kitchen on the drawing board you'll want to give a lot of thought to cabinet placement, style, and interior elements.

In placing the cabinets, work to achieve the most effective floor plan and work-center arrangement (see pages 6–7). Then let your imagination take over. Manufacturers can supply you with their latest cabinet designs (see pages 78–79), or you can work with an architect, designer, or cabinetmaker to create your own. For ideas and inspiration, examine the many cabinet variations that appear throughout this book.

Cabinets are usually designated as base or wall units, but some extend from the floor to the ceiling. Depths can vary. Ends of peninsulas and corners take special thought, as do islands of cabinetry. If you prefer windows to wall cabinets, substitute low shelves or a separate pantry (see pages 42–47) for traditional wall cabinets.

Experiment with style and color. Cabinet doors can hinge open, slide, or roll; they may or may not have a visible framework; they can overlap the framing or fit flush; they can have molding or be unadorned. Pulls range from the invisible to the highly ornamental. Paint, stain, wallpaper, fabric, glass, tile, plastic, wood, and metal—all are suitable for cabinets. Your choices of color, pattern, and texture are boundless.

Cabinets: custom or prefab?

Cabinets are probably the most costly items in your kitchen, especially if you order them custom built. Custom cabinets can easily skyrocket to more than twice the price of prefabricated units.

Of course, custom cabinets offer the greatest flexibility, since they're designed and built to fill specific needs and spaces. To reduce costs, use custom cabinets only where there are unusual structural problems. Instead of having dividers built into these units, install inexpensive plastic trays and sliding shelves.

Fortunately, a wealth of ready-made, standard-sized units is available in wood, metal, plastic laminate, or a combination of materials. The best cabinets have easy-gliding drawers and adjustable shelves; many have swing-out corner storage units, pull-up shelves, and divided tray storage.

Other ready-to-go possibilities range from skinny pull-out cupboards for canned goods to tall cabinets with louvered doors that conceal an entire laundry area. It's even possible to find one large cabinetry unit with cooktop, refrigerator, and fold-down table.

Fairly new on the prefabricated market are the elegantly modern units imported from Europe. One firm offers more than 40 door styles and colors. Outfitted with vinyl-coated-wire baskets that glide out smoothly, these miracle storage pieces have a place for everything. As costly as many custom cabinets, the units are generally ordered through an architect or designer. Be prepared to wait as long as 6 months for delivery.

Louvered cabinet doors of light-colored wood provide airy effect, especially when combined with overhead plant mezzanine. Louvered doors are especially good for ventilation in hot weather; circulating air keeps packaged food fresh. Architect: James Oliver.

▲
COMBINING CABINET STYLES

Elegant smoked glass coexists well with sophisticated ridged plastic laminate. Each cabinet serves a different purpose: behind glass, display pieces attract admiration; plastic laminate doors conceal more utilitarian kitchen gear. Design: Plus Kitchens.

Also available is a new, durable wood cabinet that snaps securely together without nails or glue—a boon to the barely handy man or woman. Referred to as the 10-minute cabinet, it requires no special tools.

Buying stock sizes

Stock cabinets come in standardized sizes. Before you place your order, plan and measure very carefully. It's often wise to ask the supplier to check your measurements.

To minimize costs, use the widest cabinets available that will fit into the space. One wide unit will cost considerably less than several narrow ones.

	BASE CABINETS	WALL CABINETS
Depth	24″	12″ to 15″
Height	34½″ (allows for 1½″ countertop). Standard finished height is 36″.	12″ to 36″ (15″, 18″, 30″ are most used)
Width	9″ to 60″. From 9″ to 36″, increments are 3″; above 36″, increments are 6″.	

CABINETS
Corners call for access ideas

Angling doors diagonally across
this corner opened up space
that's often lost. Appliances and
other kitchen gear rest on
triangular shelves.
Architect: William B. Remick.

◄ FLOOR-TO-CEILING
LAZY SUSAN

Taking a good idea to its logical
conclusion, corner lazy Susan
measures 12 feet from top to
bottom. Three sections, reached
through separate doors, turn
independently of each other.
Each ¾-inch plywood tray
measures 36 inches in diameter
and has an aluminum lip.
Middle section stores most-used
equipment, bottom section is for
less-used items, and top—
reached via ladder—is for
kitchen gear that's seldom used.
Architect: William B. Remick.

Small muffin tins and cake pans have been known to disappear forever into the far reaches of base cabinet corners. If your shelves extend into an unreachable corner, you can either position a ready-made lazy Susan in the corner or store only objects large enough to grab at one end and pull out.

But when you're remodeling cabinets or installing new ones, you can solve the corner problem. If your difficult corner is on an interior wall, open the other side and you'll have built-in shelves or a cabinet for the adjoining room, too. Utilize a corner on an outside wall to hold a wastebasket or recycling bins—they can be concealed behind a kitchen cabinet door, yet be accessible from outdoors.

More corner ideas: Design new cabinets to turn the corner on the diagonal (see photographs on page 12). Eliminate the vertical center post in the corner cabinet for easier access to what's inside. Use double doors that swing outward from the corner intersection or a double-hinged door that folds out of the way. Turntables attached to a door, built into the cabinet, or designed to pull out from the corner increase access.

▲ BASE CABINET ROUNDABOUT

Typically difficult cabinet corner received special treatment: L-shaped door opens both sides of corner, and built-in lazy Susan matches cabinets. Extra-high edges on shelves prevent spills. Architect: Ron Yeo.

◀ CORNER EXPANSION CREATES PANTRY

Instead of ending kitchen with a blank wall, or two difficult cabinet corners, owners created a walk-in pantry closet. Three walls of pantry provide storage. Appliance "garage" at end of sink counter is recessed into pantry space; appliances slide out onto kitchen counter when needed, disappear later behind tambour door.

CABINETS
Pull-outs to fill almost any need

Those narrow spaces between cabinets or next to appliances cry out for specialized pull-out storage. Cans lined up one deep, flat pans and cooky sheets, pot lids, rows of packaged food, bottles and cans of spices—all are popular items to store in pull-outs.

Ranging from knife racks a few inches square to floor-to-ceiling pantries, pull-outs glide in and out on strong slides or casters.

Adding specialized pull-out storage is easiest when you're installing new cabinetry or drastically modifying old. A number of stock cabinet lines feature pull-outs; you can also have them custom-built.

More pull-out (and drawer) ideas are on pages 50–51.

▲
BAKING CENTER IN CUSTOM UNITS

Pull-out at left has two coated-wire baskets and a deep bottom bin. Solid front panel blends with the rest of cabinetry. Baking center also includes auxiliary sink and a trio of drawers for staples. Architect: Gilbert Oliver.

◀ **TALL PANTRY PULLS OUT**

Gliding smoothly on heavy-duty hardware, one of a pair of birch and alder pull-out pantries plays its part right in middle of kitchen, not off in the wings where most pantries are located. Architect: Michael D. Moyer of The Architectural Design Group.

◄ RANGE-SIDE ACCESSIBILITY

Scaled-down version of tall
pantry shown at left, this base
cabinet component puts spices
and condiments within easy
reach of cook. Narrow cabinet
with vertical dividers on other
side of range provides balance.

▲
SIDE-BY-SIDE
PULL-OUT VARIATIONS

One of these pull-outs has two
levels: top is a coated-wire rack
sized for spices; below are
generous compartments for
bottles of oil, vinegar, and
seasonings. Just to the right,
three wire baskets for produce
pull out smoothly like drawers;
closed, cabinet door
conceals them.

◄ BETWEEN REFRIGERATOR
AND SINK

Below counter level,
strategically located pull-out
combines dishtowel rack with
miscellaneous storage. High
sides around base prevent even
tall boxes from toppling.
Shallow shelves above counter
store glasses and mugs.
Architect: Paden Prichard.

WORK CENTERS
Put pots and pans near burners and oven

Whether you need a family-size stockpot to simmer soup or a tiny pan to melt butter, you'll want to have your pots and pans within easy reach of the cooktop and oven.

Many people prefer to store cookware in drawers (in fact, some ranges come with a pot-and-pan drawer). But strong drawers with sturdy slides are essential—cookware is heavy.

Pot racks hung within an arm's reach of the cook (see pages 70–73) are a decorative option, especially if your favorite pots are made from gleaming copper or colorful enamel.

For right-at-hand storage of the cookware you use most often, consider open shelves; they're more convenient for stacking pots and pans than conventional cabinets.

▲
CUBES ON BOTH SIDES

Flanked by green cubes, range is surrounded by storage. Two-compartment modules (made of inexpensive particle board) stand side by side to form each large cube. Chopping-block tops are heat-resistant, and also handy for quick slicing. Small utensils dangle from wood strip nailed to wall behind range.

**SLIDING SHELVES ▶
UNDER COOKTOP**

Pots and pans can't be much closer than this to where they'll be used. Sliding shelves disappear behind harmonizing cabinet doors.
Architect: William Zimmerman.

◄ COOKWARE LINES UP INSIDE SHALLOW CABINET

Squeezed into an oddly shaped kitchen, extra-shallow cabinet keeps pots and pans within easy reach of range and forms one leg of L-shaped cooking center. Counter over cabinet serves as small-scale bar, convenient to living room just beyond doorway.
Architect: Mark Pechenik.

◄ VISIBLE STORAGE SURROUNDS COOKTOP

Vertical divider dowels and six coated-wire bins share underburner space with two very large drawers. Casseroles and soufflé dishes fit snugly in bins; coated wire lets chef spot a needed piece quickly.
Architect: Gilbert Oliver.

WORK CENTERS

Wrap storage around the refrigerator

Containing crisp greens for salads, nutritious dairy products, chilled beverages, fresh fruit and vegetables, and frozen food of all kinds, the refrigerator is the focus for meal preparation. It makes sense to concentrate storage around it.

Refrigerators are large vertical design elements. To give the refrigerator a more built-in, cohesive appearance, put tall cabinets or a refrigerator-height series of shelves next to it.

Incorporate varied storage into the framework around the refrigerator, but leave some counter space nearby to set down grocery bags. A counter or the top of an island directly across from the refrigerator works very well; just allow room for the refrigerator door(s) to swing open.

**REFRIGERATOR FACES ▶
INTO KITCHEN,
SHELVES FACE OUT**

Relatively simple piece of cabinet construction converted this refrigerator from a freestanding appliance to a refrigerator-plus-glass-storage cabinet; in top cabinet, vertical dividers hold hard-to-store flat items. Shelves for glasses and mugs are quite shallow—about 6 inches deep—and are hidden behind tall doors.

A PLACE FOR EVERYTHING

Whether it's wine bottles, cooky sheets, or a jar of peanut butter, it fits into this compartmented cabinetry around refrigerator. Cabinets are same depth as refrigerator; when doors are shut, they're flush with refrigerator doors. Architect: John Brenneis of The Bumgardner Architects.

FREESTANDING STORAGE STRUCTURE

Freestanding unit not only camouflages back of refrigerator, but also provides attractive storage on top. Table functions as kitchen eating and sitting spot and as a place to put bags of groceries. Additional storage is tucked in underneath table. Architect: Wendell Lovett.

ISLANDS

For an oasis of storage, discover the kitchen island

If you have floor space, you can expand your kitchen storage with an island. Pack it with shelves, drawers, bins, and cabinets; extend it out with an eating counter, or let it serve as home for a sink or cooktop. Some islands are tiny, with just enough tiled surface for a hot-from-the-oven casserole. Others are very big, the capacious centers for kitchen activities.

Allow plenty of open space between an island and adjacent surfaces—4 feet of clear space is about right.

MULTIFUNCTION ISLAND ▶

As extra work surface and part-time serving counter, this island would be valuable enough. But there's more: it deflects kitchen kibitzers from work triangle and stores kitchen equipment underneath. Doors on both ends of island open for access to shelves; drawers pull out from far end.
Designers: Don and Roberta Vandervort.

◀ CENTRAL ISLAND OFFERS SPECIALIZED STORAGE

Cheerful yellow plastic laminate wraps top of this large kitchen island. Holding a huge assortment of spices, flavorings, and other cooking essentials are three shallow, island-long shelves. Cooktop with barbecue unit is located above shelves; on other side of island, sink has its own cabinet storage underneath. Architect: John Galbraith.

◀ COOKING ISLAND IS KITCHEN FOCUS

Shelves along outside of island-with-a-cooktop display casseroles and pots and pans. Cookware is conveniently close to burners.
Architect: Bernard Judge.

ISLANDS

Movable islands go where they're needed

From simple serving carts to practically permanent islands of formidable dimensions, roll-arounds add flexibility to a kitchen storage plan.

Some movable islands are so well disguised that you'll never know they move: casters can be hidden for built-in look, and the island's design can duplicate the kitchen's built-in cabinetry. You can wheel one of these islands next to a counter or appliance or even a permanent island, for extra work surface—varying your kitchen's floor plan as needed.

Small serving carts may be designed to slide into "garage" under a counter, freeing floor space completely. Serving carts can increase your available counter space and offer a classic way to transport food and dishes from kitchen to dining room and back again.

ISLAND IS PART-TIME KITCHEN BONUS . . .

Right where it's needed for chopping or mixing chores, hexagonal island sits in center of kitchen. Under tiled top is extra cabinet space; side towel bars double as handles when island is moved. In dining area, serving counter ends on the diagonal, with glassware storage below. Wood grille panel is opened to connect kitchen with rest of house.
Architect: William Patrick.

▼

. . . PART-TIME ▶ BUFFET COUNTER

A quick rearranging and serving counter is one island longer and party-ready. Tiled tops match, as does cabinetry. Grille panel is closed to screen view of kitchen.
Architect: William Patrick.

◄ MORE THAN A SIMPLE BUTCHER BLOCK

Look beneath lavish array of gleaming cookware and see an island that is basically a butcher block table fitted with casters. Modified to include a lift-out metal bin with cover, sliding tray, wire basket, and even towel pegs, island moves from one kitchen work center to another.
Architect: Peter W. Behn.

▲ ROLL-AROUND MULTIPURPOSE CART

For flower arranging—or any other purpose—this cart rolls out to become a work island. Shelves and drawers provide storage. When bouquets are in vases, tuck cart into its home underneath counter.
Design: Plus Kitchens.

APPLIANCES
Housing the handy portables

MIXER STAYS ON ▶ SWING-UP SHELF

Heavy mixer stays put on shelf that swings up almost to counter level. When not in use, shelf (still horizontal) swings down into cabinet. In right foreground, knife holder is attached to inside of cabinet door.
Architects: Buff & Hensman.
Interior designer: Regina Mirman.

ELEGANT WOODWORK SHELTERS APPLIANCES

Used instead of wall cabinets, counter-level storage compartments preserve windows and add look of fine furniture to working kitchen. With doors closed, all you see is beautiful koa wood (inlaid dark strips are East Indian rosewood). Pivoting on side screws and washers, cabinet doors tip back into interior, out of the way. Architects: Larson, Lagerquist, and Morris.

▼

metimes, small appliance storage involves no more
an pushing a blender into a corner. But with the pro-
eration of kitchen appliances, counters can be overrun
no time with toasters, coffee makers, can openers,
icers, blenders, and food processors. Less-used small
ppliances—waffle irons, slow-cookers, and pasta mak-
s, for example—may not be out on the counter, but
ey still need to be easy to reach.

Where do you keep all these marvelous machines—
t in the open on shelves? Behind closed doors? Tucked
vay in high storage?

For answers, consider small cabinets, deep drawers,
in-out shelves, and built-in compartments. All help

keep equipment at hand but out of sight. With special
hardware, small appliances can glide out, pop up, or
swivel out and back in again.

A long parking strip at the back of a counter can provide space for all the gadgets and appliances you use
daily; a row of electrical outlets adds to the convenience.
You can even close in the space between wall cabinets
and countertop with doors that pull down, slide across,
push up, fold, or open on simple hinges.

Or consider hiding small appliances behind shutters
or screens: in a country kitchen, a row of low shutters
with fabric inserts; in a more formal kitchen, a small but
beautiful folding Oriental screen.

NITS POWER MULTIPLE ▶
PPLIANCES

ailable in several styles,
wer units are space savers.
Power pack is mounted flush
th counter surface. Tray under
unter pulls out and holds a
d processor, blender, mixer,
d bowls in specially molded
mpartments. Blades, disks,
d beaters are stored in rack
inside of door.

Even less apparent is
dercounter drawer that stores
t only equipment, but also
wer head. Deep drawer is
ounted on metal drawer
des. Power is supplied
ough a short length of
ielded flexible cable entering
m back of drawer.

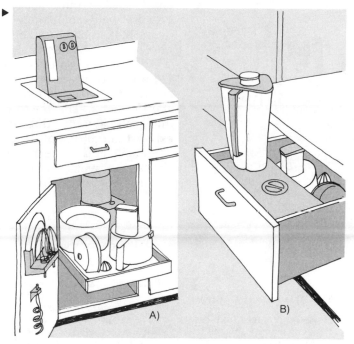

A)

B)

TAMBOUR DOOR
COMPARTMENTS

Nearly every small appliance
you own can be kept out of
sight in these 12-inch-deep
countertop compartments.
Tambour door panels work like
a roll-top desk. Thin fir slats on
linen backing slide up and
down in grooves cut into sides
of 16-inch-high compartments.
Architects: Zinkhan-Tobey.

▼

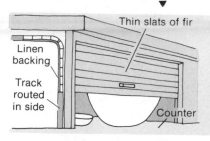

Thin slats of fir

Linen
backing

Track
routed
in side

Counter

AILORED FOR TOASTERS ▶

sily accessible, toaster oven
countertop has its own
nvenient electrical outlet.
ll-out unit over cutting board
s ready and waiting for
shly sliced bread or muffins,
des back in when not in use.
r perfect compatibility, locate
ead drawer under a toaster's
-out compartment.

APPLIANCES

Making space for the not-so-portables

A serious consideration facing the buyer of a microwave oven, convection oven, or other heavy appliance [is] where to put it so it won't gobble up much-needed counter space. If you're rebuilding or remodeling [a] kitchen, you can design built-in spaces for large pieces [—] oven, meat slicer, electric mixer—that are too heavy and unwieldy to carry from cabinet to counter.

In existing kitchens, install slide-out trays or special lift-up devices, or park heavy appliances on a utility cart and roll them to a convenient spot.

Because microwave ovens are heavy and need a [lot] of space, most owners prefer to have them built into [a] wall or cabinet. Before building a niche for a microwave, note its dimensions and weight. Most microwaves are between 17 and 20 inches deep, so placement in a standard 24-inch-deep base cabinet is simple. On the other hand, placing a unit above the counter is more difficult because wall cabinets are usually only 12 to 15 inches deep. Make sure the cabinet is sturdy enough to support the oven's weight.

Additionally, all microwave ovens require from ¾ [to] 1½ inches of space on all sides to draw in and exhaust air. Read the installation instructions carefully for exact specifications. The microwave models designed to [fit] into wall cabinetry directly over a cooktop include [an] exhaust fan and light.

Smaller and more portable than microwave ovens, convection ovens are usually not built in permanently. Put them on a counter or on a cart.

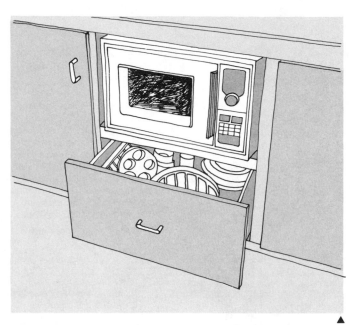

REBUILD A BASE CABINET

Door was removed from base cabinet and strong shelf added for oven; deep drawer fits underneath.

**◄ OVEN ENCLOSURE ►
ON OUTSIDE WALL**

Inside, microwave front is flush with kitchen wall; outside, enclosure matches house exterior. Both heavy box enclosure and electrical conduit leading to it are waterproof. Architects: Zinkhan-Tobey.

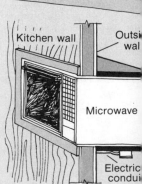

RECESSED MICROWAVE ►

Partially recessed into a wall, microwave oven sits underneath wall cabinet. Space between bottom of oven and counter below can accommodate an extra cabinet. Oven extends to back of generous wall framing, allowing front of oven to fit flush with cabinets. Architects: Singleton-Pollock and Associates.

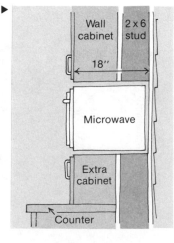

◄ USE AND STORE APPLIANCES IN PREPARATION CENTER

Food preparation center includes metal-lined bin for staples, spice shelves, and back-of-the-counter storage for large mixer and electric pasta maker. Folding doors are optional.

◄ CUT CORNER OF ROOMY CABINET

Keep your appliances, large and small, in one capacious cabinet. Cut off corner of an ordinary base cabinet, exposing wide shelf space for easy access. Two doors conceal array. (Countertop will have to be refinished.)

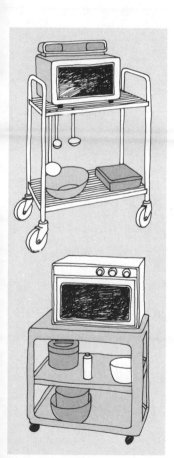

▲ PUT AN APPLIANCE ON A UTILITY CART

Both in style and size, sleek convection or microwave oven fits well on either of these high-tech utility carts. Shelf space on carts is added bonus.

CLEANUP

Around the kitchen sink

Is the counter around your kitchen sink or the cabinet under it a jumbled catchall for sponges, dishcloths, scouring pads, dishwashing detergent, and cleanser? Do you have to pull out several items before you spot the one you're hunting for?

Here are some pointers to help you organize your around-the-kitchen-sink storage:

• Keep the counters around your sink as clear as possible so they'll be free for preparing food and stacking dishes.

• Hang dishtowels and dishcloths inside the undersink

cabinet on a slide-out bar or swing-out rack.

• Hang your dish drainer under the sink on two hooks attached to the inside of the cabinet; lean the drainer tray against the cabinet wall.

• Attach a paper towel holder to the inside of the undersink cabinet door.

• Keep cleaning equipment and supplies off the cabinet floor; put them in racks, on shelves, or in plastic stacking bins.

• Measure the plumbing and the available space under your sink before buying or building storage items.

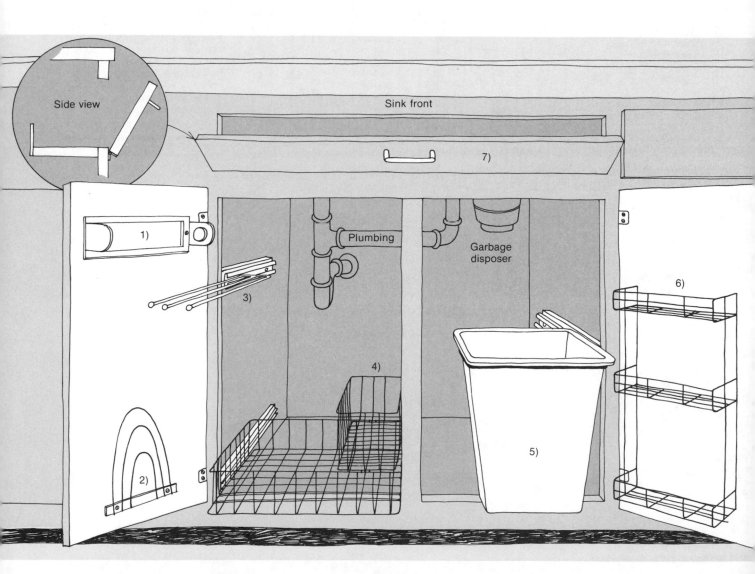

◄ STORAGE DRAWER BEHIND MOCK CABINET DOORS

Mock doors under kitchen sink are actually the front panel of a huge, undersink storage drawer that pulls out on metal slides. Drawer bottom and sides are ½-inch plywood cut to fit undersink space. Allow space in back and on each side for mounting heavy-duty, full-extension drawer slides (follow manufacturer's instructions). Existing doors or a panel custom cut to match kitchen cabinets are glued and screwed to side pieces and drawer bottom. Cutaway sides let in air and light and increase accessibility.

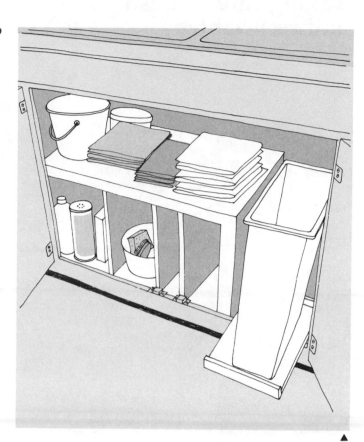

UNDERSINK STORAGE ACCESSORIES

These storage accessories fit inside undersink cabinet and keep sinkside equipment organized. Some of these accessories are easy and inexpensive to construct; others can be purchased at hardware stores or kitchen cabinet showrooms.

1) Metal or plastic paper-towel dispenser is mounted to side of cabinet door.

2) Wire or plastic rack on door holds bags.

3) Metal rack for towels slides out on track mounted to side of cabinet.

4) Sliding rack for cleaning supplies is made from vinyl-coated wire; clip-on basket can be moved to fit around plumbing.

5) Pull-out metal rack for wastebasket glides out on side-mounted track.

6) Door-mounted rack with three shelves is available in vinyl-coated wire, plastic, or metal; or construct your own from wood.

7) Long, shallow shelf behind false front of sink organizes brushes, scrubbers, and sponges.

CONTAINERS ELIMINATE ► UNDERSINK CLUTTER

Plastic dishpan and stacking bins can help you organize undersink clutter. Plastic caddy keeps cleaning supplies neat and portable.

▲ BUILT-IN UNIT FOR UNDERSINK CABINET

Built-in shelf with vertical dividers below can be custom fitted for your needs. To design this simple unit, place sheet of paper on cabinet floor and position on paper all cleaning supplies regularly stored under sink; determine divider widths and shelf height. Construct unit from wood, using plan as a construction guide. Consider installing a sliding shelf for wastebasket.

CLEANUP

Taking care of trash and recyclables

Efficient and orderly ways of dealing with kitchen wast[e] can put an end to messy, overflowing wastebaske[t] unpleasant trash odors, and some of the drudgery [of] garbage duty.

Place your kitchen wastebasket in an accessible sp[ot] near where trash is generated. Once you locate all t[he] waste production points in your kitchen, such as the c[an] opener, food preparation counter, or chopping bloc[k] you may find, as many people do, that the best pla[ce] for the wastebasket is under or near the kitchen sin[k.]

Always line your wastebasket with a heavy-duty gr[o-] cery bag or plastic liner. Your wastebasket will st[ay] cleaner, and your trash will be more likely to make [it] outside to the garbage can in one uneventful trip.

Not all kitchen waste ends up in the wastebask[et.] Much will go down your sink's garbage disposer. So[me] kitchens are equipped with trash compactors that c[an] compress what would fill three to four 20-gallon ga[r-] bage cans into one odorless, leakproof, disposable ba[g.]

If you're a gardener, you may want to keep organ[ic] kitchen wastes in a separate container to add to a co[m-] post pile. And if you have room in your kitchen, y[ou] can put recyclables in separate receptacles to save so[rt-] ing time later on. Aluminum and tin cans (flattened[),] glass bottles and jars, newspapers, and paper bags a[re] all recyclable.

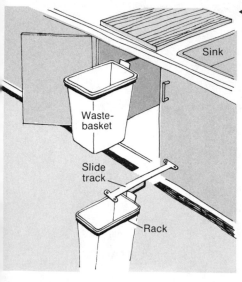

◀ PULL-OUT WASTEBASKET

Wastebasket slips into metal ring holder that pulls out on slide track fastened inside undersink cabinet. In extended position, wastebasket can be lifted out of holder for emptying; it slides into cabinet when not in use.

Sink

Waste-basket

Slide track

Rack

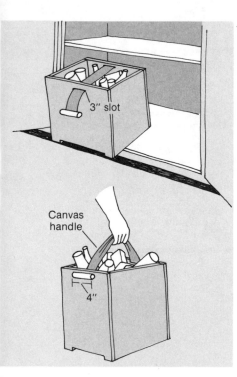

3" slot

Canvas handle

4"

◀ PORTABLE BOX FOR RECYCLABLES

Portable plywood box keeps bottles, cans, and papers handy but out of the way. Store box in a base cabinet or on a shelf, or in a convenient spot near kitchen door. When box is full, lift it by the handle and load it into your car for a trip to the recycling center.

Make box from ¾-inch plywood to fit your own specifications. Cut narrow 3-inch slots in opposite sides about 1½ inches from top for handle; make handle from heavy-duty canvas, allowing an extra 4 inches for slack. Feed handle through slots and attach ends securely with heavy-duty staples to stops made from 4-inch lengths of dowel 1 inch in diameter. Sand and finish.

Cabinet door back

▲ WIRE RACK FOR UNDERSINK DOOR

Use inside of undersink cabinet door to mount waste rack made of vinyl-coated wire. Plastic liner or small wastebasket can be used in rack.

TIP-OUT WASTE BIN

You can deposit and unload waste easily with a tip-out waste bin. When opened, full storage space is exposed so it'[s] easy to reach to bottom. Unit can also be fitted with a wastebasket.

For bin to tip forward, back must be lower than front (see illustration). Build sides, bottom, and back from ½-inch plywood; match front to kitche[n] cabinetry.

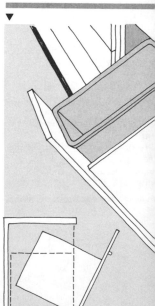

Hinge

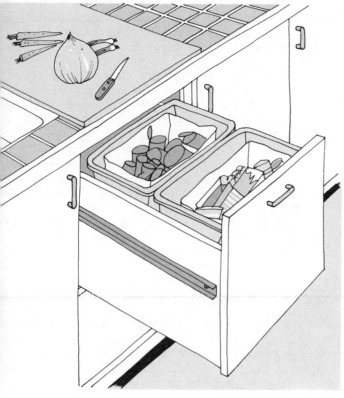

◄ DUAL-DUTY DRAWER

Underneath the kitchen sink isn't the only place to put a wastebasket. Here, a pull-out for wastes and recyclables is located directly below cutting board so food scraps can easily be swept off into it. Height of drawer saves bending.

Drawer can be fitted with two plastic wastebaskets: one for wastes and one for recyclables. Grocery bags can be stored in any remaining space in back of drawer.

Sides, back, and bottom of drawer are built from ½-inch plywood; front matches kitchen cabinetry. Drawer pulls out smoothly on metal slides.

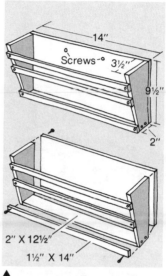

THREE WASTEBASKET DESIGNS

When plumbing in undersink cabinet interferes with placement of wastebasket, look for a specially designed one; or opt for a covered container you can keep out on kitchen floor.

A) Step on the pedal of this wastebasket and lid springs up.

B) Here, lid locks open and leaves your hands free.

C) Cutaway wastebasket fits under plumbing in kitchen sink cabinet. Use grocery bag for liner.

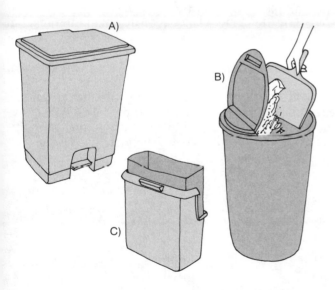

▲ GROCERY-BAG RACK

Attached to inside of a cabinet door, rack provides organized storage for grocery bags.

To make rack, cut two 9½-inch-long end pieces from a 1 by 4 board. Taper them so they are 3½ inches wide at top and 2 inches wide at bottom. Cut three 1½ by 14-inch front slats and a 2 by 12½-inch bottom piece from ½-inch plywood. Cut a 9½ by 14-inch back from ¼-inch plywood or hardboard.

Glue and screw side pieces and bottom to back, and slats to side pieces. Sand and finish; attach to inside of cabinet door with screws.

SHELVES

Open or closed storage?

Chances are, a look into a professional kitchen in a restaurant or hotel will reveal the whole *batterie de cuisine* positioned for convenience on open shelves. Pots line up in graduated sizes; spices, knives, and mixing bowls are only a reach away, as carefully organized as the instruments in an operating room. The cooks can find what they need easily and can tell at a glance what needs to be reordered.

In home kitchens, too, the trend toward open shelving is growing, partly because we are all becoming more aware of food and its preparation, whether it's how to put a food processor to ultimate use or how to spin out ribbons of tender pasta.

Many people feel increasing pride in keeping all the implements of good cooking right out on display, with bright labels, packages, and pans adding color to the open shelves. "Now this is a *cook's* kitchen" is what you hear when someone sees all the utensils, crockery, cans, and bottles stored in plain sight. The whole room has become sort of an extended pantry with the cook's personal tastes in food and equipment on view. In short, it's a kitchen of character.

The practical side of shelving

Other practical reasons explain the popularity of open storage. Shelves are less expensive than traditional cabinets and drawers, and are easy to install. They can be permanent, built-in units constructed integrally with a new kitchen, or they can be made simply with boards and brackets or even with prefinished, precut kits that come complete with hardware for hanging.

Not only are shelves less expensive than cabinets, but they're also often portable (a boon to renters) and can be rearranged easily. You can usually adjust the height of shelves to accommodate large items or seasonal storage.

In addition to wood, shelf materials include metal, heavy plastic, glass, particle board protected with polyurethane and outlined with wood strips to prevent chipping, and sturdy vinyl-coated wire. Edging strips can

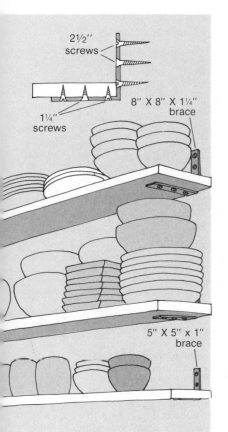

2½'' screws

1¼'' screws

8" X 8" X 1¼" brace

5" X 5" x 1" brace

▲

USE L-SHAPED BRACES FOR SUPPORT

Open shelves rest on L-shaped corner braces (angle irons). Fasten braces to wall studs with 2½-inch-long screws, then fasten shelves to horizontal part of braces with 1¼-inch screws. Wide shelves are 2 by 10s attached to 8 by 8 by 1¼-inch braces; narrow shelf is 2 by 6 held by 5 by 5 by 1-inch braces.

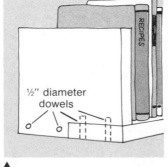

½'' diameter dowels

▲
SPILLPROOF END PIECES

Simple end piece secures items on open shelf. Cut end piece in L-shaped lap to fit a corresponding cut in shelf. Four dowels, each ½ inch in diameter, are glued in—two into end and two from underneath.
Architect: Donald Erdman.

CONSIDER INDUSTRIAL ▶ SHELVING

Freestanding or anchored to a wall, industrial shelving is hard-working and indestructible. Made of metal and sometimes available in bright colors, high-tech shelves can solve many kitchen storage problems. Team these units with coated-wire or plastic baskets and stacking bins, or see-through plastic or glass storage containers.

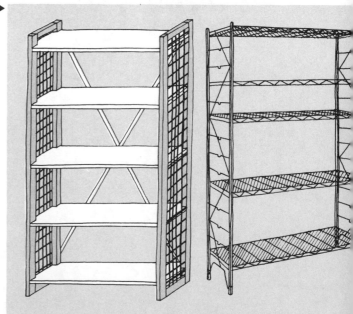

conceal undershelf lights. Shelves can be suspended from the ceiling, supported on a counter, screwed directly into a wall, or supported by metal tracks and brackets, braces, dowels, or clips; or they can be part of freestanding units.

But is it for me?

The opened-up kitchen clearly is not for everyone. Dust on dishes not often used, general disarray, and a daily confrontation with tomato soup cans are simply not tolerable to everyone.

Closed cabinets, on the other hand, conceal everything. Dishes, food, and ordinary clutter can be cleared off the open counters, leaving the traditional neat and orderly kitchen cherished by many cooks.

If you're ready to trade in your traditional closed cabinets but are unsure about that out-in-the-open living, one solution is to build shelves like conventional cabinets—but leave off the doors. Later, if you decide you want a closed-up kitchen, simply add doors. Or consider a combination of cabinets constructed with doors (to hide the real embarrassments) and without.

ABOVE-THE-SINK OPEN SHELVES

Casseroles and cook books, coffee makers and canisters—all of these kitchen items and more are accommodated on open shelves. Boxlike shelves match wood countertop, contrast pleasantly with white cabinets and walls.
Architects: Richard Strauss and Kathleen H. Strauss.

▼

SHELVES

Open shelves in the kitchen— easy to see, easy to reach

Depending on your kitchen's floor plan, you can locate open shelves almost anywhere. Often they're hung against a wall, alternating with or replacing the cabinets; but they can also be suspended from the ceiling, built into an island, or tucked in between wall studs.

Shelf style is up to you. From the multitude of choices, consider shelves with lips to keep breakable glassware and ceramics from sliding off, or very shallow shelves to store spices or teacups one deep in space that otherwise might not be used. Whatever shelf style you choose, make sure the shelf material is easy to clean.

Throughout this book you'll notice many different shelves—and any number of places to put them. For more ideas, refer to the *Sunset* books *Bookshelves & Cabinets* and *Wall Systems & Shelving*.

OPEN CABINET HANGS ▶ OVER KITCHEN ISLAND

Striking oval cabinet suspended from ceiling above cooking/ dining island is accessible from every side. Concealed at bottom of cabinet are cooktop light and exhaust fan. Coordinating open cabinets against wall take place of traditional closed wall cabinets. Shelves in these units adjust to hold everything from coffee mugs to a tall ceramic pitcher.
Architect: Robert C. Peterson.

▲
CURVED DESIGN MAKES CORNER MORE ACCESSIBLE

These double-curve, open cabinets are attractive alternative to both conventional cabinets and conventional shelving—and their design makes corner space much more accessible. Compartments keep good-looking kitchen articles on display and handy for frequent use.
Design: Plus Kitchens.

◀ IF YOUR DISHES ARE TOO PRETTY TO HIDE . . .

Why hide a favorite pottery collection behind cabinet doors? All you need are stained wooden shelves and an expanse of wall to create a stunning kitchen display area like this one.
Architect: Bill Kirsch.

SHELVES

Shelves in unexpected places

Adding a shelf or two to your kitchen may seem like a relatively small step to take in improving your storage, but it can make a big difference in saving you time and motion.

Focus on the work centers (see pages 6–7): tuck shelves above the cooktop, ovens, refrigerator, or sink; cover the side of an appliance with a series of shallow shelves. Shelves against a window can mask a less-than-perfect view; light, in turn, enhances the objects on the shelves. Stack up shelves in a corner where walls would otherwise be bare.

Scrutinize available walls for shelf possibilities, but make sure that cabinet doors will swing freely after shelves are installed.

STRIKING SOLUTION FOR A TIGHT CORNER

Where no space exists for a traditional wall cabinet, open shelves just fit between window and doorway. Enclosed in a wooden frame, unit is not only handy but also very attractive. Exterior is painted blue to match kitchen cabinets; bright white interior provides sharp, clean contrast. Metal tracks and clips make top shelf adjustable. Cabinet designers: Woodward Dike and L. W. Grady. Interior designer: Phyllis Rowen of Rowen and Mentzer.

CREATE A SPARKLING ▶ WINDOW DISPLAY

Tempered glass window shelves display flowers, plants, potted herbs, and bric-a-brac. Especially suitable when your view is less than picturesque, shelves can be adjusted to any height by moving metal support brackets along tracks on sides of window frames.

SPICE SHELF ▶
UNDER CABINET

This handy spice shelf—actually an extension of handsome oak cabinets above—stretches 8 feet, the full length of cooktop counter. Stored one-deep, spices are easy to see and reach. Architects: Wagstaff & McDonald.

◀ SHELVING UNIT
OVER PASS-THROUGH

Located over pass-through between food preparation and dining areas, wooden shelving unit makes storage space accessible from both sides. Unit is screwed securely to ceiling beams and has wooden slats on the bottom for hanging stemmed glassware. Architect: John O'Brien of O'Brien & Associates.

SHELVES

Supplement counter space with accessible shelves

In many kitchens, the backs of the counters fill rapidly with assorted jars, small appliances, cook books, and fruit bowls, encroaching on precious food-preparation space.

But where is there another place as convenient as the countertop for the assorted paraphernalia? A shelf or two close to counter height can do the trick.

CORNER LEDGE ▶ IS CUSTOM-MADE FOR COFFEE MAKER

Previously unused corner is now permanent home for automatic drip coffee maker, thanks to handy ledge built on the diagonal. Above it, oak cabinet with glass-paneled doors is also on the diagonal to make corner more accessible and allow space behind it for coffee maker's wiring and plumbing.
Architect: Richard Hahn.

ELIMINATE ▶ COUNTER CLUTTER

Shelf units on countertops actually create more space for food preparation because they hold kitchen gear that would otherwise clutter counters. Extra height of shelves helps to divide kitchen and living area on far side, yet room retains feeling of openness.
Architect: Richard Sygar.

**◄ HANDY SHELF
DISPLAYS COOK BOOKS,
BRIGHTENS COUNTER SPACE**

Cook books and metal canisters-are off counters and out of the way, but still within easy reach on this handy shelf. Fixtures mounted to underside of shelf light baking counter below. Architects: Fisher-Friedman Associates.

**▲
ADD INTEREST—
AND STORAGE SPACE**

You can maximize your work space by displaying decorative items on eye-catching staggered shelves rather than on kitchen counters. Shelves are made from plastic laminate edged with wood.
Architects: Sortun-Vos.

**▲
RECESSED MINI-SHELVES
DESIGNED FOR SPICES**

Recessed shelves 3½ inches deep keep spices within easy reach of cook, yet off counter work space.
Architect: Peter W. Behn.

PANTRIES

Fitting in a mini-pantry

The pantry in grandma's house was stocked with enough food to last for weeks on end. But with the scarcity of extra space in today's homes, most of us don't have the luxury of a separate, built-in pantry.

It is possible, though, to tuck a small pantry ingeniously into your kitchen so you can buy in quantity when prices are low and cut down on your trips to the grocery store. Small pantries bring food storage out of standard cabinets and into specially designed compartments. In an effective pantry, food is easy to see and easy to reach.

PANTRY CABINET PUTS UNUSED CORNER TO WORK

Custom-built wooden mini-pantry fits into corner between sink and oven, a space that might otherwise be wasted. Shelves are shallow to provide visible and accessible single-row storage of canned goods and condiments—and to make room for extra storage on inside of each door. Pretty ceramics find a home on top of unit. Architect: Woodward Dike.

▼

◀ DOUBLE-DECKER PANTRY OVERHEAD

Plastic laminate doors of two-tiered overhead cabinets slide instead of opening out into head space. Upper level, 5 inches deeper than lower level, holds large pans. Doors of lower level add a cheerful splash of color to predominantly white kitchen.
Architect: Wendell Lovett.

◀ STEPS PROVIDE UP-FRONT STORAGE

Nothing gets lost in the back of these cabinets. In unit on left, spices line up on graduated storage steps, keeping entire inventory visible at a glance. One compartment in divided cabinet on right has three steps for jars and packages.

Paper towel holder under cabinet is out of sight, but towels are within easy reach.
Architect: Gilbert Oliver.

PANTRIES

If you have space to spare, plan a walk-in pantry

Whether it's a tiny closet or a real room, a walk-in pantry gives you a complete overview of your provisions and plenty of room to store them. If you're a canning or preserving buff, what could be more gratifying than surveying rows of colorful ready-for-the-winter fruits, pickles, jams, and jellies? Even supermarket packaging can be enjoyed as a display of eye-catching designs.

With a light inside the pantry you'll have a clear view of the line-ups of canned goods and paper products. A surface, such as a small table or handy ledge, is convenient for setting down bags and boxes of groceries as you restock the pantry.

NARROW ALCOVE CALLS ▶ FOR SHALLOW SHELVES

Painted with black semigloss, these long, wooden shelves transform a narrow alcove into a mouth-watering display of home-canned foods. Thanks to metal tracks and brackets, shelves can be adjusted to any height.
Architect: Michael D. Moyer of The Architectural Design Group.

WELL-PLACED APPLIANCE ▶ TURNS OPEN SHELVES INTO WALK-IN PANTRY

Refrigerator turns area of open shelves into pantry that's easily accessible, yet partially closed off from view. Shelves are lined with checkered, vinyl-coated shelf paper that's cheerful and easy to wipe clean.
Architects: Larson, Lagerquist, Morris.

JOINT VENTURE IN ▶ WINE AND FOOD STORAGE

Convenient walk-in pantry features wine "cellar" on far wall and a cooler to keep wines at proper temperature. Tripod holds uncorking device. Pantry shelves are fixed at various heights; stock pot and party-size coffee maker fit on counter. Ladder brings top shelves within reach.
Design: Gordon Grover.

◀ THIS ONE HAS IT ALL

Walk-in pantry has everything you could want in kitchen storage. Shelves on walls adjust (using metal tracks and clips) to accommodate kitchen equipment of all different heights; hooks hold baking molds and small cooking utensils. Packaged foods and canned goods fit in single rows on shallow door shelves. Especially convenient are counter for preparing food and storing appliances, undershelf baskets for fruits and vegetables, and storage place for stool.
Architects: Sortun-Vos.

PANTRIES
Floor-to-ceiling storage

If there's no room in your kichen for a large walk-in pantry, what better place to store edibles and other kitchen essentials than in a floor-to-ceiling pantry near one or more of your work centers?

A pantry near your range or cooktop would make top-of-the-stove cooking a breeze; a tall cabinet near your oven could hold casserole and baking dishes (and the ingredients that go into them); and a pantry near the refrigerator would be a convenient spot for sleepy heads to find breakfast foods such as cereals, bread, and jam. Whatever they store, floor-to-ceiling pantries maximize space, minimize steps, and look like a million!

WORK-CENTER STORAGE ▶

Built-in pantry in warm, dry spot next to oven keeps cereals, crackers, and other foods crisp. Sugar, cooking oil, condiments, and canned goods in pantry are only a reach away from food preparation counter.
Architects: Richard Strauss and Kathleen H. Strauss.

RECESSED SHELVES ALLOW STORAGE ON DOOR

Both inside of door and bottom half of tall end-of-counter cabinet are lined with pegboard for hanging up baking and cooking paraphernalia. Top half of cabinet features recessed shelves for spices and condiments.
Architects: Buff & Hensman. Interior designer: Regina Mirman.

▲
SEEING DOUBLE

Attractive twin pantries with U-shaped shelves display tableware, crockery, baskets, cook books, spices, and brightly packaged foods behind sparkling glass-paned doors. Architect: Marshall Lewis.

PANTRIES

The larder—updated

The larder is an old-fashioned idea that's worth a second look. The handsome built-in storehouses featured here are great for cooks who like to stockpile canned and packaged foods when they're on special at the supermarket or who buy large quantities of their favorite fruits and vegetables at height-of-the-season prices.

If your larder is primarily for fresh produce, it's best to keep it cool and dark. Use wire shelves or vents to the outdoors (cover them with fine window-screen mesh) to keep air circulating, and avoid storing any bruised or damaged produce.

◀ FLEXIBLE CABINET STORES ASSORTMENT OF FOOD

Sparkling white double doors swing open to reveal a flexible food storage system. Tall bottles of soda and a big basket brimming with oranges fit in capacious drawers. Mounted on metal slides, drawers have so much room above them that they serve as pull-out shelves as well. There's even room in them for plastic stacking bins. Shelves above drawers adjust on metal tracks to accommodate jumbo-size food packages.
Architects: Fisher-Friedman Associates.

SHELVES GLIDE OUT ▶ FOR EASY ACCESS

Cabinet door next to top oven is actually front of four-shelf unit that pulls out on metal slides; bottom cabinet houses two handy slide-out shelves. Both units provide quick access to food and very visible storage.
Architect: Michael D. Moyer of The Architectural Design Group. Interior designer: Joan Simon.

EVEN DOORS ARE MINI-PANTRIES

Spacious yet compact pantry features U-shaped shelves that make sure nothing is ever out of sight and forgotten. Shelves adjust to accommodate everything from packages of nuts and cereals to small appliances. Even the double doors provide storage space; bottles and canned goods on door shelves fit one-deep, keeping labels visible. Trash compactor and water cooler occupy separate compartment. Cabinet designers: Woodward Dike and L. W. Grady. Interior designer: Phyllis Rowen of Rowen and Mentzer.

▼

A WHOLE WALL OF KITCHEN STORAGE

The beauty of these cabinets lies in their natural finish, clean lines, and almost unlimited storage capacity. Spacious shelves behind cabinet doors hold packaged food, canned goods, and dishes; vented tip-out bins are filled with fruits and vegetables; space between cabinets and ceiling stores large baskets and crockery. Architect: Robert C. Peterson.

DRAWERS

Sizes, shapes, and styles for every kitchen need

Drawers are storage on the move—efficient container that slide out to display their contents, then slide i again, out of the way. They can match or complemen any kitchen decor and hold just about everything.

Custom drawers are expensive, but they do provid specially designed storage; they also carry through th style of the rest of the cabinetry. Much less costly ar stock drawers, which are available in standard sizes a most building supply centers; these, too, can be custor fitted for particular uses (see pages 50–51).

Building your own drawers can be economical, bu it's one of the most exacting of all cabinetry projects Skill in woodworking is required for all but the simples box design that merely pulls out from a shelf withou slides or runners.

If you do decide to build your own, be sure to pla carefully, investigate all the available types and sizes o hardware, and keep in mind this rule of thumb: a drawe shouldn't be much deeper than 30 inches (the length o a long arm) or much wider than 3 feet (or it'll be awk ward and heavy to open, even with sturdy handles o both sides).

◄ KICK-SPACE STORAGE

These prefabricated drawers fit under specially designed base cabinets to make good use of a space that's usually lost. Floor-level drawers provide children with easy access to toys and drawing supplies; or they might store picnic utensils, garden gloves, a supply of dishtowels, or any number of other things. Design: Plus Kitchens.

**INTERIORS ARE ►
SPECIALLY DESIGNED**

Handy, custom-made food preparation island features butcher block counter and drawers with custom interiors. Slanted racks in shallow drawers keep entire inventory of spices visible; deep drawer holds several knife blocks. Design: Gordon Grover.

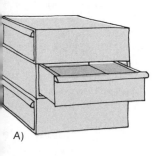

A)

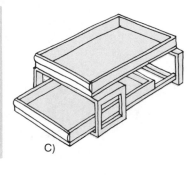

B)

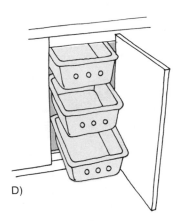

C)

D)

VERSATILE READY-MADES EXPAND STORAGE

Ready-made plastic drawers expand storage space in a jiffy and bring a clean, bright new style to the kitchen.

A) Among the most versatile are freestanding stacking drawers that interlock. Made in individual units, they can be piled up so all drawers open in the same direction—or in different directions.

B) This special drawer unit screws in under a wall cabinet. Also available is a deeper version for one or two loaves of bread.

C) Space that's often wasted between shelves can be put to use with a neat stack of two slide-out drawers on their own supports. Widely available, they're sold in 12-inch and 16-inch widths.

D) Plastic trays, working like drawers, slide in and out on a rack that fits into a cabinet at least 15 inches wide.

OPENING DRAWERS WITHOUT HARDWARE

The high cost of good-looking hardware makes these drawer-opening ideas valuable. None uses hardware; all are easy to make.

A) Simplest pull is a hand hold. Half circles cut out of tops of drawer fronts provide firm openers.

B) Finger holes drilled in drawer fronts have rustic look. For finger comfort, round edges of holes with a beading bit in a router.

C) Hardwood caps fit over edge of plywood drawers. A cap or other pull attached to a drawer immediately under a counter should extend out 3½ inches; 2½ inches will do for pulls on lower drawers. All have finger grooves routed on undersides. Caps are first glued, then nailed.

D) Ribbons of maple decorate the plain fronts of plastic laminate drawers. Rout a finger recess on top and bottom of wood strips before screwing them into place.

DRAWERS

Dividers to organize drawers and tip-outs

Dividers in drawers are great organizers, creating distinct spaces that bring order out of chaos. With drawer dividers you can put your hands immediately on the items you need, as well as put them back more easily. Though you may already have drawer dividers for tidying silverware, consider using them for organizing baking and cooking utensils, pot tops, even food staples

Many cabinet manufactures now offer drawers with dividers as part of their stock cabinetry. But using basic carpentry tools, you can customize your existing drawers with dividers; or you can purchase divided trays or baskets made of wood, plastic, vinyl-coated wire, and straw. Also available in many different sizes are interlocking plastic organizers you can make into whatever configuration you need in your drawer.

Simple cardboard or metal boxes can maintain order in your kitchen drawers. Even a shoe box can be a drawer organizer. Removable or portable drawer dividers are easy to clean and relocate.

▲
CUSTOM COMPARTMENTS FOR BAKING UTENSILS

Spatulas, measuring spoons, beaters, cooky cutters, and other baking tools stay in tiptop order in this divided drawer.

Cut liner pieces for all four sides of drawer from ½-inch plywood. Cut grooves in front and back liner pieces to accommodate lengthwise dividers made from ½-inch plywood. Cut grooves in side liner pieces and in lengthwise dividers for ¼-inch hardboard crosswise dividers.

Place liner pieces against sides of drawer and slide lengthwise and crosswise dividers into place; glue if desired. Sand and finish.

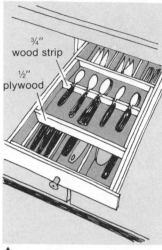

▲
SPLIT LEVEL SILVERWARE DRAWER

Resting on plywood side pieces, silverware tray on top lifts out or slides so utensils underneath can be reached.

From ½-inch plywood, cut four liner pieces to fit inside drawer, allowing room for 1½-inch-deep tray to sit on top. Cut grooves in front and back liner pieces for ¼-inch dividers. Glue liner pieces to drawer. Cut dividers to fit into grooves. Sand and finish.

To construct lift-out tray, cut a bottom piece (wide enough to rest on liners) from ¼-inch plywood. From ½-inch plywood, cut four side pieces 1¼ inches deep. Assemble tray with glue and nails. Cut wood strip from ¾-inch plywood and make grooves that will hold silverware as shown. Sand and finish.

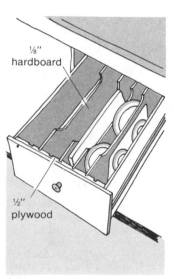

▲
VERTICAL DIVIDERS

Dividers in a deep drawer provide practical storage for hard-to-store shallow items—small baking pans, muffin tins, pot tops, and trays. Dividers can be removed for occasional cleaning and adjusted to accommodate larger items.

Cut an equal number of corresponding ⅛-inch grooves in two ½-inch plywood pieces. (Cut more grooves than needed so dividers can be adjusted.) Glue pieces inside drawer. Make dividers from ⅛-inch hardboard. Cut away top edge of each divider (see illustration). Sand and finish. Rub a bar of soap on ends of dividers so they'll slide more easily into grooves.

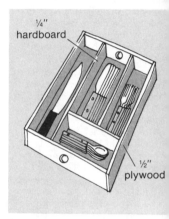

▲
EASY-TO-MAKE SILVERWARE TRAY

Here's a removable insert to keep everything in its place in your silverware drawer. Constructed from ½-inch plywood and ¼-inch hardboard, tray calls for only very basic carpentry skills.

Cut four side pieces from ½-inch plywood. Drill holes in two end pieces to serve as handles. Glue and nail pieces together. Cut bottom from ½-inch plywood, and glue and nail to side pieces. Cut dividers from ¼-inch hardboard; glue and nail into position (drill pilot holes for nails). Sand and finish.

DIVIDED TIP-OUT BIN

Handy dispenser for staples such as flour, sugar, and rice opens at an angle so you can easily reach to the bottom. Potatoes and onions can also be stored in such a bin if there are holes for ventilation.

Make bin from ¾-inch plywood. Inside can be lined with metal or covered with plastic laminate. Attach bin to cabinet with piano hinge along bottom. Attach metal drawer stop or chain to top edge at back to keep bin from opening too far.

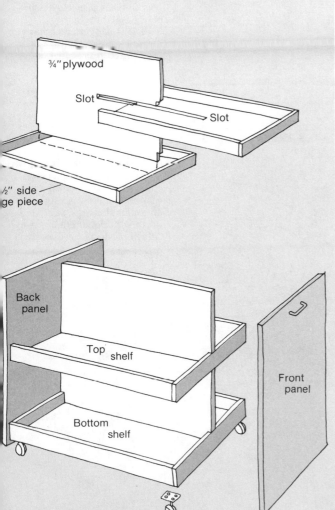

TWO-LEVEL UNIT ON CASTERS

Kitchen paraphernalia can be kept within easy reach in this four-compartment storage unit that slides under a counter when not in use.

Construct it from ¾-inch plywood; use glue and nails to join pieces.

Cut vertical divider as shown in illustration, adding ¾-inch-wide slot for top shelf. Cut bottom shelf piece and attach 2½-inch-high edge pieces. Attach divider to bottom shelf.

Cut top shelf with ¾-inch-wide slot halfway through board. Attach 2½-inch-high edge pieces to front and sides of top shelf. Slide top shelf slot into slot in vertical divider as shown; glue and nail into place. Attach front and back panels with screws. Sand and finish; mount on casters.

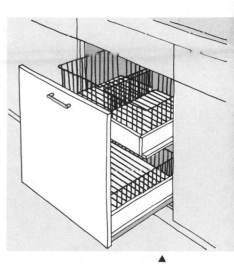

COATED-WIRE BINS

Removable bins in pull-out keep fresh vegetables separate and provide optimal ventilation. Here, bottom bin is attached to drawer front; top bin operates on its own slides.

RACKS AND HOLDERS
. . . for knives

Knife storage requires some special thought. First, there's safety to consider. Throwing knives into a general utensil drawer can easily result in nicked fingers. Second, knives stay sharper when they don't bounce around in drawers or on countertops.

A simple knife rack answers both concerns; so does a specially designed cutlery drawer—and both are great organizers. Some of the attractive and functional knife racks shown here are available in department, cookware, and cutlery stores; others are easy do-it-yourself projects.

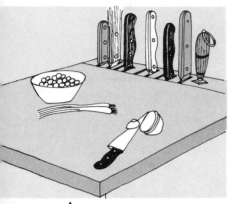

▲ KNIFE SLOTS IN BUTCHER BLOCK

You can store your knives right where you'll use them most if you incorporate knife slots into a butcher block table or countertop. Simply drop knives into slots, and your entire cutlery collection is at your fingertips.

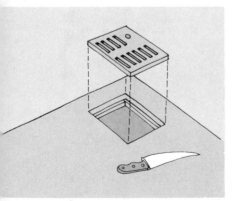

▲ REMOVABLE SLOTTED RACK

Custom-made slotted rack fits flush with cutting board but can be removed easily. For safety, use ¼-inch plywood to cordon off area inside cabinet where blades will hang down.

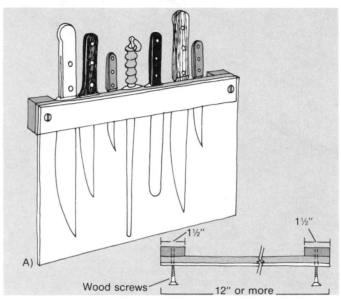

A) Wood screws   1½"   12" or more   1½"

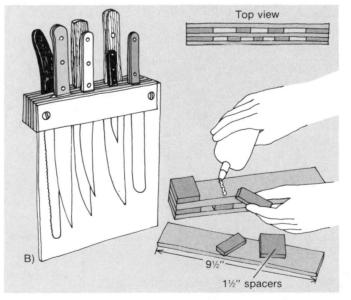

Top view

B)   9½"   1½" spacers

◀ HANGING KNIFE RACKS

Hanging racks are convenient for knife storage and easy to make. Attach them to a wall, cabinet, or edge of a butcher block table using 3-inch-long screws. Panel of clear plexiglass can be added to front of either rack to shield knife blades.

A) Assemble this rack from a 1½ by 12-inch (or longer) hardwood strip and two 1½-inch wood pieces. Using glue, attach small pieces to ends of hardwood strip and clamp. Sand and finish with polyurethane sealer. Attach plexiglass, if desired.

B) This hanging rack has two rows of knife slots; it's constructed from 4 feet of hardwood flooring that is 2 inches wide and $5/16$ inch thick. Cut flooring into three 9½-inch pieces, four 1½-inch pieces, and five ¾-inch spacers. Glue a 1½-inch piece to each end of one long piece, then add three spacers. Glue another long piece on top, and add two remaining 1½-inch pieces to ends; attach two remaining spacers. Glue third long piece on top, and clamp. Sand and finish with polyurethane sealer. Attach plexiglass, if desired.

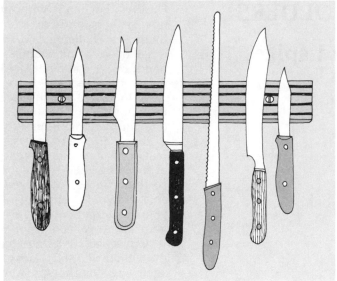

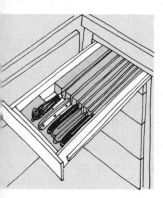

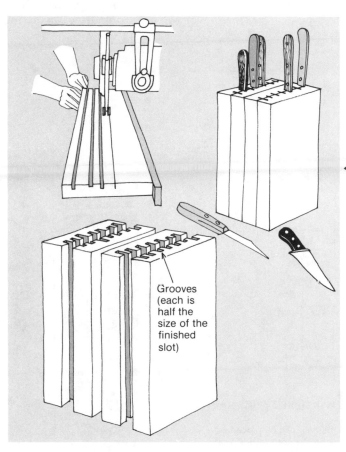

Grooves
(each is
half the
size of the
finished
slot)

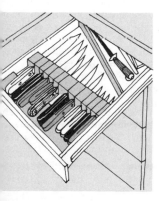

◄ MAGNETIC-STRIP KNIFE RACK

Like magic, magnetic-strip rack attracts steel knives and holds them securely in place. Available at department, cookware, and cutlery stores, rack is a solid wood piece with inlaid magnetic strips. Attach to wall or outside of cabinet using a screw at each end. You can also place magnetic-strip rack in a drawer.

◄ MAKE YOUR OWN KNIFE BLOCK

Sturdy block keeps your entire cutlery collection organized— and portable. Use a 4-foot length of 2 by 8 of any clear wood.

Cut grooves down entire length of board. Number, width, and depth of grooves depend on size and number of knives you're storing. (Here, seven grooves form 14 slots; remember that finished slots will measure twice the depth of grooves.)

Cut board into four equal lengths. With grooves aligned, glue pieces together to form two rows of slots, and clamp. Sand and finish.

CUSTOMIZING YOUR CUTLERY DRAWER

A cutlery drawer keeps knives handy, organized, and stationary. Some cabinet manufacturers offer special cutlery drawers, but you can make such a drawer yourself quite easily.

Cut wood the same width and half the length of inside of drawer. Make a series of grooves for knife blades in board. Glue to bottom of drawer; add thin piece of wood where knife handles rest. Sand and finish.

KNIFE ORGANIZER FOR DRAWER

A simple grooved strip works well in a kitchen drawer. Cut 2-inch wood strip the width of your drawer. Along strip make grooves for knife blades. Glue strip to drawer bottom, and glue thin piece of wood where knife handles will rest.

RACKS AND HOLDERS
. . . for herbs and spices

Hardly a kitchen is without a healthy collection of jars tins, shakers, and boxes of spices and herbs. Arrangin them is a challenge: on the one hand, there's a wid range of sizes and shapes to contend with; on the othe hand, many containers look exactly alike except for th name. How can you store spices and herbs so they'r close to where you use them—usually the cooktop o food preparation center—and so you're able to find th one you need without a long search?

Here's an illustrated assortment of spice racks, man making use of often-overlooked storage space. Which ever arrangement you choose, be sure to display spice so they can be recognized at a glance. Then you'll b able to avoid sprinkling in cayenne pepper when yo wanted cinnamon; you also won't have to dig throug your entire collection for the one container you need If your spice containers have a habit of walking awa from their allotted places, you may want to label th shelf edge or the spot directly behind each containe with the name of the spice stored there.

Generally, spice and herb containers should be store away from direct heat, moisture, and light. Keep th tops tightly closed between uses to prevent loss o flavor.

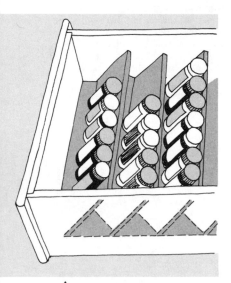

▲ ANGLED DIVIDERS INSIDE A DRAWER

You'll have little problem finding the spice you need in this custom-fitted spice drawer with angled dividers.

From ¼-inch plywood, cut four dividers, each the width of drawer and 4 inches high. Cut four triangular wood supports the width of drawer (see illustration). Sand and finish, then glue pieces into drawer.

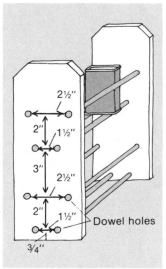

2½"
2" 1½"
3" 2½"
2" 1½"
¾"
Dowel holes

▲ TWO-TIERED SPICE RACK

This rack can be placed on a countertop or mounted on a wall. It holds jars and large tins upright, small tins at an angle. You can expand or alter rack to meet your own specifications.

Cut two 11-inch-long pieces from a 1 by 4. Cut eight 14-inch lengths from 5/16-inch dowels. Drill holes for dowels in end pieces (see illustration for positioning holes). Glue dowels in holes. Sand and finish.

◄ SPACE FOR SPICES BETWEEN THE STUDS

When there's no place left in your kitchen to organize spices, don't panic. The 3½-inch-deep by about 14½-inch-wide cavitie (those not jammed with pipes, vents, or wiring) inside your walls are ripe for exploration. These cavities lie between vertical 2 by 4 studs that frame walls. Because they're out of sight, they're often overlooked.

Cut a hole in wall between two studs; then build a unit to fit opening. Use ½-inch plywood for top, bottom, sides, and shelves; use ¼-inch plywood for back. Dowels hold spices in place. Sand and finish then slip unit into wall and attach securely. Nail 1 by 3-inch trim around outside edges.

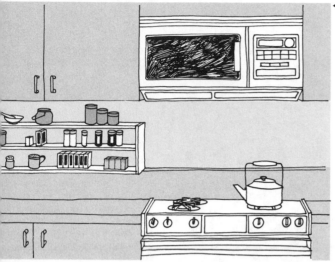

◀ BACKSPLASH SPICE SHELVES

Decorative and problem-solving, these shelves utilize space between countertop and wall cabinets. Assemble open-shelf spice unit from 1 by 6s or 1 by 4s butt jointed, glued, and nailed together. Add a ¼-inch plywood back, and screw unit to wall studs. Sand shelves and finish them to match cabinets.

TWO-SIDED SPICE RACK SWINGS OUT

Spices line up one-deep on each side of this sturdy holder; rack swings out from wall cabinet on piano hinge attached to side of cabinet. Shallow enough (5 inches deep) to permit storage behind, rack is tapered in back so it can swing clear of adjacent items.

▼

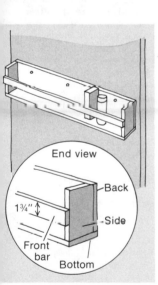

◀ DOOR-MOUNTED RACK

Tap storage potential of cabinet doors by attaching a simple wire, metal, or wood rack to inside.

To build a wood rack to your own specifications, cut back, bottom, and sides from 2¼-inch lattice; cut front piece from 1¾-inch lattice. Rack should be 2 inches shorter than width of cabinet opening. Glue and nail rack together; sand and finish. Attach rack to door using screws long enough to hold rack but short enough not to pierce door front.

End view

Back

1¾"

Side

Front bar

Bottom

Lazy Susan spice tray

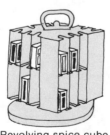

Revolving spice cube

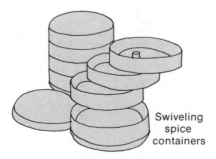

Swiveling spice containers

◀ COUNTERTOP SPICE ORGANIZERS

Keep an organizer near cooktop or food preparation area for quick access to seasonings you use most often. Easily cleaned plastic organizers like the ones shown here can be found in department, cookware, and hardware stores.

RACKS AND HOLDERS

. . . for wine

◄ STACKED TILES OR TUBES

Handsome terra cotta drain tiles about 1 foot long and 4 inches in diameter make cool, dark holders for wine. Build them in as part of kitchen construction (as shown in illustration) or simply stack them in an existing cabinet or rack.

Mailing tubes fitted snugly on cabinet shelf provide quick, inexpensive, and portable wine storage. Heavyweight tubes about 4 inches in diameter can be stacked two or three rows high.

4" diameter

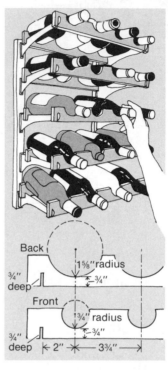

Back

1⅝" radius

¾"
deep

¾"

Front

1¾" radius

¾"
deep

¾"

2"

3¾"

◄ BRACKETS SUPPORT BOTTLE HOLDERS

Readily available bookshelf tracks and brackets form sturdy skeleton of wall-mounted bottle rack that's especially suited to narrow space.

Plan rack so you can mount tracks directly to wall studs (usually about 16 inches apart); use long wood screws for maximum strength.

Front and back wooden holders are 1 by 2s; oiled walnut is a good choice if rack is to be on display. Small and large cutouts cradle bottles.

Placement of 10-inch bracket depends on size of bottles. Good spacing for easy removal of standard-size bottles is 3½ inches between top of one holder and bottom of holder above it. Caution: Make sure brackets are fitted securely into slots in tracks.

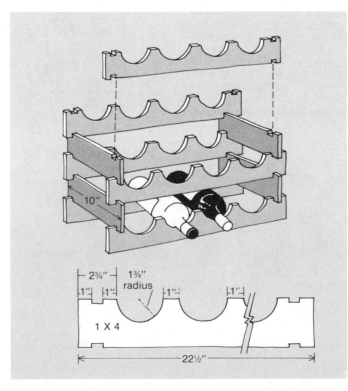

10"

2¾"

1¾"
radius

1" 1"

1"

1"

1 X 4

22½"

◄ STACKING RACKS

Add sections to wine storage unit as needed.

Cut half circles in pine 1 by as shown; sand. Cut cross-lap notches ⅜ inch deep and ¾ inch wide on upper and lower edges of boards. On both edges of 10-inch connectors, cut slightly undersized notches, then sand until they fit tightly with matching notches; assemble and stack.

These racks are designed for shelves about 23 inches across but can be built wider or narrower—just increase or decrease number of half circles for bottles and 1-inch spaces in between.

Few homes have a cool underground vault where wine bottles can repose in a carefully controlled atmosphere. But wine can be kept quite nicely in the kitchen—if you plan your wine storage area carefully.

Above all, a steady temperature is important. Wine cannot tolerate radical shifts between warm and cold, but it will keep satisfactorily at any relatively even temperature between 45° and 75°F/7° and 24°C. Never place a wine rack next to an oven or a drafty doorway. Instead, choose a dark, quiet place close to the floor, away from sunlight and the vibrations of machinery and slamming doors. It's also important to store bottles on their sides; if corks dry out and shrink, air can seep in and spoil the contents.

Whether you're thinking in terms of an entire room designed especially for your wine collection, or merely a small unit to fit inside a kitchen cupboard or on an open pantry shelf, there's a wealth of stacking racks, storage boxes, and folding racks to buy or build.

If you are (or would like to be) a serious collector of wines, you might consider relocating your brooms and converting the closet to a wine "cellar." With careful planning, a small closet can hold several hundred bottles of various sizes. To circulate air and maintain a constant, ideal temperature (around 60°F/16°C), a refrigeration unit with a fan can be installed in the ceiling.

On the other hand, if storing jug wines is your only problem, you're in luck. Usually meant to be used soon after purchase, jug wines can be placed in an upright position nearly anywhere that's cool.

More ideas for storing wine in or near the kitchen are pictured on pages 19 and 43.

◄ LENGTHS OF PIPE INSIDE CABINET

Custom storage unit features wine cabinet, shelves for dishes, and built-in hot tray for buffet serving. Wine bottles rest in glued-together 6-inch lengths of PVC pipe. Larger bottles slide into compartment underneath. Architect: Gilbert Oliver.

DINING AREAS
Creating an eat-in kitchen

If you don't have a large eat-in kitchen but would like to set up a special area where your family can have breakfast and lunch (or dinner on the run), look to your kitchen island, base cabinets, or other storage units. Tuck a few stools around a cooking island and it becomes a short-order lunch counter; establish a separate dining area using a storage-shelf room divider; create a ceramic-tile snack bar at the end of a kitchen counter, or add a tabletop to convert a corner base cabinet into a breakfast nook.

Use the cabinets and drawers under, over, and around your new eating area to store glasses, plates, silverware, and the small appliances you like to have nearby at mealtimes—a toaster or coffee maker, for instance.

▲
**CORNER TABLE
WITH STORAGE
ABOVE AND BELOW**

Built around brick chimney, corner table seats three for breakfast. Storage pedestal supplements glass-doored cabinets full of dishes. Architects: Sortun-Vos.

**SHELVES NEXT TO ▶
BREAKFAST TABLE**

Attractive shelves, crammed with cook books, food magazines, and kitchen-related miscellany, separate breakfast table from rest of kitchen. On kitchen side of divider is cooktop with pot and pan storage beneath. Through doorway at far end of kitchen is separate dining room. Architect: William Zimmerman.

◄ DROP-LEAF COOKING ISLAND

With cooktop in center of cooking/eating island, food won't get cold in this kitchen. Drop leaves on two ends extend work surface, and stools can slide underneath on three sides. Overhead unit houses stereo speakers, plant lights, and illumination for cooktop. Architect: John Brenneis of The Bumgardner Architects.

◄ CABINETS FRAME KITCHEN DOORWAY

Just behind counter extension, series of green-painted cabinets extends around doorway. Side cabinets are convenient for storing everyday things; overhead ones are for less-in-demand items. Cabinets with white louvered doors add even more storage space along display wall.

DINING AREAS

The pass-through connection

You use dishes, silverware, and glasses in the breakfast area or dining room, but wash them in the kitchen. Where's the best place to store these things, and how can you most conveniently move them from one room to the other?

A pass-through is the answer to both questions. You expect it to provide the convenience of handing food and dishes directly into the eating area. But taken a step further, a pass-through can offer a world of storage.

At its simplest, a pass-through is just an opening in a wall or divider. A counter on either the cooking side or the eating side (or both) increases a pass-through's practicality.

You can fit in shelves, cabinets, and hooks below, above, or on the sides of a pass-through. Storage you can reach into from both the kitchen and the eating area is a great way to save steps. In deep pass-through dividers, install sliding shelves or drawers that pull out from two sides to make the storage more accessible.

▲ SEE-THROUGH CABINET ABOVE OPEN COUNTER

Circles cut in orange plastic laminate behind sliding plexiglass panels show off dishes; shelves are open on kitchen side. Cabinet doors underneath also slide, eliminating problem of clearance.
Architect: Wendell Lovett.

◄ STORAGE PASS-THROUGH SERVES EATING AREA

This handsome pass-through links enclosed patio and kitchen. Glassware is displayed behind small-paned cabinet doors overhead; drawers and cabinets fill undercounter space. Auxiliary sink serves dining area.
Architect: Woodward Dike.
Interior designers: Phyllis Rowen, Suzanne Bryson.
Cabinet designer: L. W. Grady.

TWO-WAY CHINA CABINET ▶

Doors and drawers of this pass-through can be opened from both sides. Replacing a solid wall, pass-through made both kitchen and dining area seem larger. Rooms are brighter, since glass cabinet doors and pass-through let light pass between areas.
Architect: Robert Arrigoni of Backen Arrigoni & Ross, Inc.

COUNTERTOP COMPARTMENTS

Big enough to hold a favorite set of dishes, these sliding-door compartments are accessible from dining room on far side of pass-through as well as from kitchen. And no counter space is lost: tops of compartments form a shelf.
Architects: Buff & Hensman. Interior designer: Regina Mirman.

▼

◀ SLINGS FOR SILVERWARE

Threaded around narrow blocks of wood, very fine plastic window-screen mesh forms pouches for silverware. Seamed to leave long edges finished and smooth, then seamed again to flatten, mesh's double thickness provides strength. Cloth can be substituted for mesh.

TABLEWARE AND LINENS

Keeping treasures on display— or hidden away

Displaying beautiful dishes, glassware, and silver is ha[lf] the fun of having them. Open shelves or a glass-doore[d] china cabinet let you admire your treasures betwee[n] meals—and when it's time to use them, you can run a[n] instant inventory of table-setting possibilities.

Table linens—less likely to be on display—are mos[t] convenient if they're stored near the table. Everyda[y] placemats and napkins can be kept in a handy drawe[r] or on an open shelf; tablecloths can be hung from dow[els] els that swing out, glide out, or are stacked across

**ANTIQUE AUGMENTS ▶
BUILT-IN STORAGE**

A world of dining storage is offered here. Dishes and table linens fill antique china cabinet at left; casseroles, baskets, groceries, and more dishes occupy shelves behind tall, narrow doors. Shallow cupboards are recessed into dining area wall. Interior designer: Joan Simon.

shallow cabinet. If there's no space to hang your table-cloths, you can keep wrinkles to a minimum by rolling them around large mailing tubes and giving the rolls plenty of room in a drawer.

You may want to add some secure storage for especially valuable items such as silver. One idea for this is a compartment behind a false kick-space panel (see page 76). Wherever you put silver, enclose it in layers of flannel or special tarnish-retardant cloth to block air flow and cut down on the need for polishing.

CUSTOM CUPBOARDS FIT DINING NEEDS

Everything from table leaves to coffee cups is kept in floor-to-ceiling cupboards along wall separating dining room from kitchen. Table leaves fit between blocks of wood nailed to top and bottom of tallest cupboard compartment. Extra folding chairs, also divided by blocks of wood, stand in compartment sized for them. Shelves fill in remaining cupboard space. Design: Pennington & Pennington.

◄ SHALLOW DRAWERS FOR TABLE LINENS

Stack of shallow drawers is concealed behind a cabinet door until it's time to set the table. Low shelf fronts make placemats highly visible and act as pulls when selection is made. Architect: Bo-Ivar Nyquist.

BASKETS OF COATED WIRE IN TWO-WAY CABINET

Easily visible through coated wire, dishes can be removed from both sides of two-way cabinet. Placemats and napkins lie flat in adjacent drawers. Cabinet is well located, standing between informal eating area and formal dining room, with kitchen to one side.
Architect: Gilbert Oliver.
Interior designer: Nancy Brown, ASID.

TABLEWARE AND LINENS

Keeping dinner table items in the kitchen

In more and more homes, the "good" china and table linens are finding their way into the kitchen. One reason for this is today's more casual lifestyle: the kitchen is often the setting for family dining—and sometimes even for entertaining. Another reason is that many newer homes have small dining areas instead of formal dining rooms, and there's simply no space in them for storage.

Luckily, the kitchen is full of possibilities for storing and displaying tableware and linens. Just use your imagination! Keep a service for twelve on sliding shelves in a versatile base unit that doubles as a buffet; conceal a half-dozen tablecloths behind a movable cabinet that looks built-in; or turn traditional wall cabinets into a stunning display of china and glassware by substituting glass-paned doors for solid ones.

COUNTER BUFFET FOR KITCHEN ENTERTAINING

Base unit below windows runs full length of kitchen. Strong sliding shelves hold heavy plates, yet glide out smoothly. Closed, cabinets have a handsome, tailored look. With buffet set up, dried flower arrangement separates serving area from cooking area. Architect: Woodward Dike.

◄ NEXT-TO-THE-DOOR DISH STORAGE

Proximity to dining room was a priority here, so tableware is stationed near doorway. Small-paned glass cabinet doors show off china, silver, and crystal on tempered glass shelves. Backs of cabinets are simply the kitchen walls (note vertical groove pattern) painted white. Designer: L. W. Grady.

MOVABLE CABINET CONCEALS LINENS

Cabinet with microwave oven on top just *looks* built-in. Moved away, cabinet reveals table linens hanging—wrinkle free—from smoothly finished boards. Spice rack pulls out sideways so it's accessible even when microwave cabinet is in place. Auxiliary sink and warming oven share stationary cabinet at right.
Architect: Jane Hastings of The Hastings Group.

WORK AREAS / OFFICES

Make space for hobbies and other activities

All kinds of activities go on in the kitchen besides cooking: flower arranging, sewing, ironing, appointment making, gift wrapping, and art projects are just a few of them. If you want to keep your papier-mâché away from your boeuf bourguignon, plan a kitchen hobby area with plenty of appropriate storage.

Consider adding an auxiliary sink if you do lots of flower arranging or other projects requiring water. Put the sink and accompanying storage (drawers for scissors and deep shelves for vases, perhaps) outside the kitchen work triangle.

WELL-CONCEALED ▶
KITCHEN LAUNDRY

Sophisticated European fir
cabinetry with black plastic
laminate counters hides a pull-
out ironing board and, in tall
cabinet next to board, a washer
and dryer.
Architect: Gilbert Oliver.
Interior designer: Nancy Brown,
ASID.

COUNTER IS OUTSIDE
WORK TRIANGLE

Plenty of cabinets and large
drawers under butcher block
work surface store materials for
flower arranging, gift wrapping,
other projects. Work counter is
at one end of kitchen, out of
sink-range-refrigerator work
triangle.
Architects: Richard Strauss and
Kathleen H. Strauss.

WORK AREAS/OFFICES

Space for a tiny desk or a complete office

Probably the most obvious uses for a kitchen desk are meal planning and shopping-list writing—good reason to have the desk convenient to the pantry. Space for recipe files and cook books is important; so is room to spread out the newspaper's supermarket specials. You may want to include space for a calculator and type writer, too—not to mention a home computer.

Many people like to have a telephone in the kitchen so they can answer calls while they cook. Sometimes this expands into a message center, with an appoint ment calendar, blackboard or bulletin board, and intercom.

◀ KITCHEN ISLAND DOES DOUBLE DUTY

Stepped down from food preparation height to desk height, island does double service. Desk's design provides space for chair, telephone connection, and file drawer. Desk end of island is away from focus of meal preparation. Architects: Fisher-Friedman Associates.

◀ **PART-TIME DESK, PART-TIME COUNTER**

Sometimes it's occupied with menu planning or schedule organizing; at other times, entire counter is taken over for baking or serving. With wall phone at one end, mixer on hinge-up shelf at other end, book shelves above, and chair space below, this counter is ready for any use.
Architect: William Zimmerman.

UPDATING A ROLL-TOP ▶

Traditional advantages of a roll-top desk—quick concealment of projects-in-process, convenience of having everything still in place when you return—are retained in this built-in kitchen desk. New appeal comes from its unobtrusive location around the corner from kitchen work area, yet close to pantry cabinets. Style and materials of desk match rest of cabinetry.
Architect: Robert C. Peterson.

TELEPHONE'S TUCKED INTO ISLAND

Long, narrow niche in this oak island conceals wall phone. Bank of drawers is handy for telephone books, pencil, and paper; expansive island top provides work surface.
Designer: Alison Ruedy.

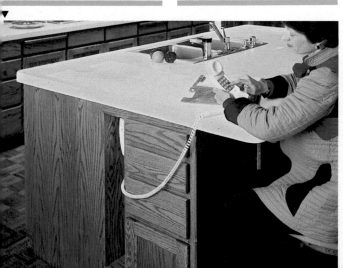

KITCHEN HANG-UPS

Find a strategic spot to hang up kitchen gear

Your kitchen may already have lots of places to attach hooks and hangers: under cabinets, over pipes, or directly to ceiling beams or wall studs.

If not, you can find or build any number of devices that create a framework on which to put hooks and hangers: metal or plastic grids, perforated hardboard or plastic, latticework, and custom or commercial pot racks.

Wherever you put your hooks and hangers, you'll want your tools low enough to reach but high enough to avoid bumps on the head. It's best to plan around the height of the cook in your household. Also, make sure hanging storage won't block the swing of cabinet doors or obstruct access to shelves.

LADDERLIKE POT RACK

Tiny 12-volt lights shine on sparkling copperware hung from horizontal "ladder" with copper tubing rungs. Oak frame extends around sides of range hood. Brass S-hooks were purchased at a marine supply store.
Architect: Kathleen H. Strauss of Don Olsen Associates.

DOWEL RUNS ALONG WALL

Supported every 3 feet by track-and-bracket hardware, 2-inch-thick dowel runs parallel to long wall. S-hooks slip over dowel to hold cooking gear.
Architect: Richard Sygar.

PLASTIC WALL HANGERS

Accessories are stored around cooktop on four different wall-hung units: a spice rack, a potholder hook, a small utensil bar, and a food processor accessory rack. White plastic hangers harmonize with kitchen's soft gray and white color scheme.
Architect: Guy McGinnis.

▼

▲
◄ **BASKETS ABOVE PENINSULA COUNTER**

Visually dividing kitchen from breakfast area, basket collection accents ceiling beam. On kitchen side, S-hooks slip over flat iron bar attached to side of beam. On wall, antique utensils hanging on nails include an English pan scraper and a fork for catching eels.

KITCHEN HANG-UPS

From modest pegboard panels to sleek high-tech grids

Are countertop appliances, gourmet cookware, dinnerware, and utensils eating up valuable work and storage space in your kitchen? Overcrowded countertops and full-to-overflowing cabinets and drawers are a common problem.

Hanging devices can help you turn almost any vacant surface—ceilings, walls, cabinet doors and sides, the undersides of shelves and wall cabinets—into extra storage space. These hanging devices include simple hooks, baskets, shelves, wall units such as grids and perforated hardboard (pegboard), and racks for ceilings, walls, and cabinet doors.

Hanging devices offer tremendous versatility. Many can be moved as the need arises; many can be modified with components such as shelves, bins, and hooks; and most can accommodate a wide assortment of items, from produce to paella pans.

Fasteners—whatever you use to attach a hanging device to the wall or ceiling—are another consideration. They must be capable of supporting the weight of the items that will be stored—as well as the weight of the device itself. A sizable pot rack, for example, with a cook's collection of pots and pans, weighs a good many pounds. Also, some fasteners work better for certain holding jobs than others. So be sure you read manufacturers' suggestions carefully when choosing from the array of suction, magnetic, stick-on, screw-in, and nail-in hooks and fasteners, as well as such heavy-duty fasteners as togglebolts, expansion bolts, and sleeve-type anchors.

Remember, too, that when you use hanging storage devices in your kitchen, whatever you're storing will be in plain view. For an organized effect, group objects according to their function, shape, or size.

WALL DISPLAY ▶
OF POTS AND PANS

As pleasing to look at as they are convenient to use, shiny copper and copper-bottom pots and pans decorate white wall next to cooktop.

PEGBOARD PULL-OUTS FOR POTS AND PANS

Functional—and easy—solution to cabinet full of disorganized pots and pans is one or more ¼-inch pegboard panels that slide loosely between 1 by 2s screwed to top and bottom of cabinet. Cut each panel slightly smaller than height and depth of cabinet. Attach a small knob near front edge of each panel so it can be pulled out easily.

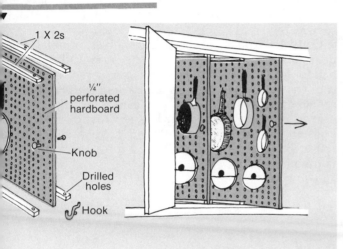

1 X 2s

¼" perforated hardboard

Knob

Drilled holes

Hook

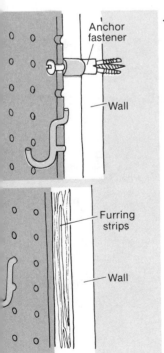

Anchor fastener

Wall

Furring strips

Wall

◄ PERFORATED PANELS FOR A MULTITUDE OF USES

Perforated hardboard, also called pegboard, is perfect for wall storage. Though you may associate it with tool storage in the garage, pegboard works equally well on kitchen walls, especially if it's brightly painted and edged with molding.

Purchase pegboard panels from hardware or lumber stores. Attach them to wall on 2 by 2 wood furring strips screwed into wall studs; or use sleeve-type wall anchor fasteners with spacers that hold panels slightly away from wall to allow clearance in back for hooks.

Another similar and versatile wall storage system is plastic, pegboard-type panels with components that hook on—shelves, bins, knife holders, and hooks. System can be screwed to wall vertically or horizontally.

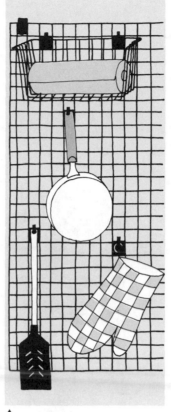

▲
HIGH-TECH GRID

Vinyl-coated or chrome wire grid panel lets you hang utensils, cookware, paper goods, and foodstuffs on racks, shelves, bins, and special hooks. Panel is either screwed directly into wall or clipped onto fasteners screwed into wall. Grid can also be suspended from ceiling on long hooks.

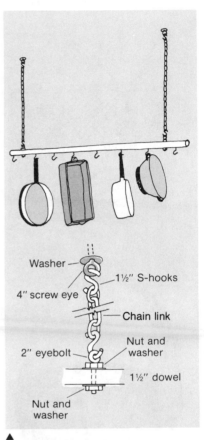

Washer

1½" S-hooks

4" screw eye

Chain link

2" eyebolt

Nut and washer

1½" dowel

Nut and washer

▲
SUSPEND POT RACK FROM CEILING

Simple pot rack frees cupboard space in kitchen where storage is at a premium. To construct this lightweight rack, attach row of screw hooks to 1½-inch-thick dowel. At each end, drill hole and insert 2-inch eyebolt, nuts, and washers (as shown). Use S-hooks and metal chains to suspend dowel from two 4-inch screw eyes secured to ceiling joists (usually 16 inches apart). Adjust rack to convenient height.

KIDS' CORNERS

Play area storage

Children love to be in the kitchen. After all, most of them have spent a lot of time there sitting in a highchair, crawling on the floor, banging on pots and pans.

Because they're around the cook so much, kids need a section of the kitchen where they won't be underfoot or exposed to the dangers of steaming pots and sharp knives. To separate *your* work from *their* play, locate the children's area where the traffic patterns of play and cooking don't constantly cross.

In a large kitchen, it's fairly easy to child-proof one end and set aside places to draw pictures and scatter toys. Small kitchens with more limited storage require tighter planning.

Design your children's activity center for their convenience. Toddlers need to have their playthings on low open shelves; older children enjoy a small desk for drawing or counter space for their own culinary concoctions.

Consider adjustable racks and shelves of metal, plastic, or wood. Short, movable shelves on wall tracks are handy for an older child; one can serve as a work counter. A stack of drawers can be made available to the growing child successively, starting from the bottom drawer and moving upward. Keep toys organized in pull-out bins or baskets. If you have available wall space, hang a cork board nearby for art work and favorite pictures.

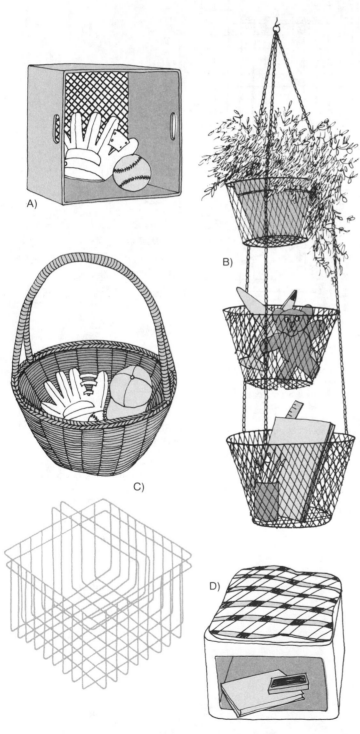

A)

C)

B)

D)

◄ **"RIGHT NOW" STORAGE**

There comes a time in every parent's day when toys and projects must be cleaned up— the faster, the better. Then kids and parents alike will appreciate simple storage units like the ones shown here. Consider **A)** inexpensive plastic boxes, **B)** hanging three-tier wire mesh baskets, **C)** baskets with handles, or **D)** sturdy plastic cubes.

Cubes and boxes can be stacked conveniently and pushed under a counter out of the way. Some cubes double as low stools with storage compartments underneath.

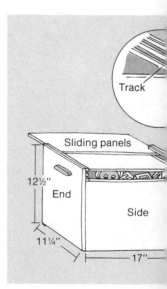

Track

Sliding panels

End

Side

12½"

11¼"

17"

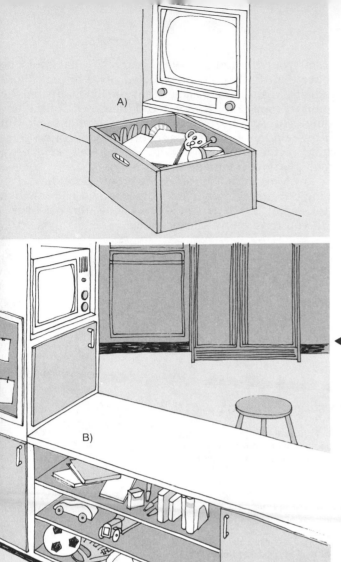

TELEVISION GARAGES

For television watching in the kitchen, place TV where kids can see it and not be underfoot.

A) Kids will appreciate television parked low (about a foot above floor) in a cubbyhole of a base cabinet; arrangement features a pull-out toy box underneath. Leave enough space around TV to pull out or adjust set.

B) If you're remodeling, build TV niche over divider between kitchen and dining area; screen is visible not only from kitchen and counter seats but also from play area.

PLAYTIME MINI-CART

Cart with three or four stacked baskets moves easily from kids' rooms to kitchen and back again, conveying a full playday's supply of trucks, stuffed animals, games, and books. On some carts, baskets pull out for easy access.

DRAWING-SURFACE TOY BOX

Toddlers can stow toys inside portable box and use cover as a drawing table. From ½-inch plywood, cut two side pieces 17 by 11 inches, and two end pieces 11¼ by 12½ inches. Attach handles to end pieces. Make grooves by gluing and nailing three ¼-inch-square by 11¼-inch-long wood strips to top inside of both end pieces. Allow enough space between strips for panels to slide easily.) Cut bottom to fit. Using nails and glue, assemble box with ends overlapping sides.

From ¼-inch hardboard or plywood, cut two cover panels 11¼ by 16⅞ inches. (They'll slide apart to make a good-size drawing surface.) Sand and finish.

DISCOVER SPACE UNDER A SHELF, ON A WALL

Even if your kitchen's layout limits active play, a few of your children's quiet-time toys can be kept within reach. **A)** Two-story rack of vinyl-coated wire steals little wall space. **B)** Pocketed wall organizer hangs over desk or work counter. **C)** Hang-up canvas bag holds bulky toys. **D)** Shelf of vinyl-coated wire slips into place beneath existing open shelf. Roomy enough for books and drawing materials, wire shelf is easy to relocate.

SURPRISE STORAGE
Discovering unused spaces

When your kitchen is storage-starved, what could be better than finding an unexpected place to park those gadgets, dishes, or baskets that are lined up on the counter, waiting for a spot to call their own. Take a few minutes to scrutinize your kitchen. Observe the width of the window ledges—plants or a row of coffee mugs could go there. That blank end of the wall cabinet is a good place for a family bulletin board.

How long has it been since the broom closet held anything but clutter? Remove the door, add a wide shelf at desk height, attach narrow shelves above for cook books, and you have a tiny kitchen office.

◄ A SUSPENDED DOOR

Hanging from ceiling on nylon rope or chain, door provides lots of extra storage. Suspend door (finished to match kitchen cabinets) from eyebolts or hooks securely anchored in open beams or in ceiling joists (usually spaced 16 or 24 inches apart).

Top of door is a deck for lightweight baskets; hooks on underneath surface hold pots and pans at a convenient—and safe—height. Hooks go through door and are secured with large-diameter washers and nuts on top of door.

KICK-SPACE STORAGE

Don't let odds and ends— screwdrivers, hammer, tape, string—take up precious space in base cabinet drawers; add kick-space drawers below base cabinets for extra storage.

Suppliers of European cabinetry offer kick-space drawers that fit below their specially designed base units (see photo on page 48). In Europe, kick spaces are 8 inches high, twice their height in North America.

But even the traditional 4-inch space can be useful. Cut out a section of the kick-space panel and install a shallow drawer; fill with children's art supplies. Or conceal a tray for silver and other valuables behind kick-space panel.

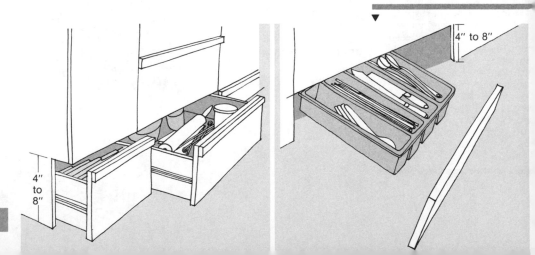

◄ MINI-PANTRY AROUND THE CORNER

Bottles, canned goods, and spices can be tucked into unexpectedly convenient spots on shallow shelves that keep labels visible.

Mini-pantry around the corner from stacked ovens (or refrigerator) is created by extending wall 6 inches beyond sides of ovens. Shelves adjust on tracks attached to inside of wall extensions.

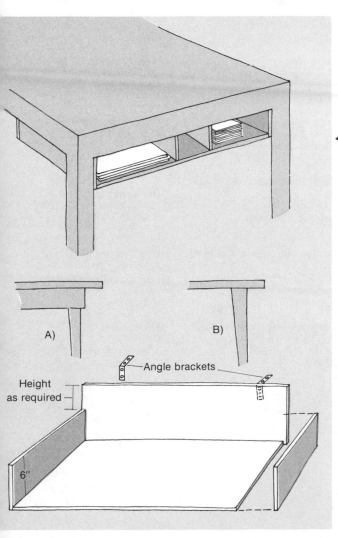

◄ STORAGE SHELF UNDER TABLE

A kitchen table is a blessing both for family meals and as an extra work surface. It's even handier with an added on storage shelf at one end for placemats, napkins, even a few dishes. Space can double as single-row wine rack.

Build bottom, sides, and back from pine shelving or ½-inch plywood. Make front opening approximately 6 inches high. Unit should be wide enough to fit snugly under top of table and against legs. Sand and finish shelf before attaching it to table.

For skirted table (A) or Parsons table, make shelf unit with a high back; use angle brackets to fasten back to underside of table. Screw sides to legs. On country-style table (B), make back same height as sides. Fasten shelf to table as described above.

To use shelf as wine rack, glue and nail wood dividers into unit to make compartments about 4 inches wide.

SOURCES

Manufacturers of kitchen cabinets and storage products

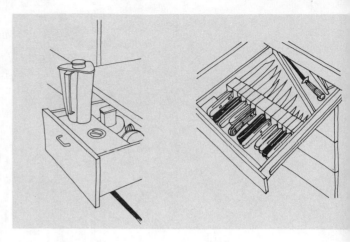

When you're trying to transform an old kitchen into one that's innovative and workable, you'll find a wealth of ideas in the brochures put out by the various manufacturers of kitchen storage units. Here's a selection of major cabinet and storage product manufacturers who will send you information on request; they can also tell you about local outlets or distributors for their products. The entries are coded to identify what each company manufactures; importers of European cabinetry are indicated as well. The product codes and addresses in this list are accurate as of press time.

The Yellow Pages of your telephone directory and the National Kitchen & Bath Association (124 Main Street, Hackettstown, NJ 07840), can help you locate kitchen showrooms, cabinetmakers, designers, architects, and other sources near you.

(C) custom cabinets
(S) stock cabinets
(SO) special order cabinets
(SP) storage products
(m) metal
(p) plastic
(pv) plastic laminate veneer
(w) wood
(i) imported

Akro-Mils
1293 S. Main Street
Akron, OH 44301
(SP/m,p)

Allmilmö Corporation
P.O. Box 629-S2
Fairfield, NJ 07006
(SO/pv,w,i)

ALNO Kitchen Cabinets, Inc.
P.O. Box 10474
Charleston Heights, SC 29411
(C/pv,w,i)

Amerock Corp.
4000 Auburn Street
Rockford, IL 61101
(SP/m,w)

Ampco
P.O. Box 608
Rosedale, MS 38769
(C/m)

AristOKraft Cabinets
P.O. Box 420
Jasper, IN 47546
(S, SO/pv,w)

Artcraft Wire Works
230 Fifth Avenue
New York, NY 10001
(SP/m)

Beck Lumber Co.
5102 S. Washington Street
Tacoma, WA 98409
(S/pv,w)

Beylerian Limited
11 E. 26th Street
New York, NY 10010
(SP/p)

Birchcraft Kitchens, Inc.
1612 Thorn Street
Reading, PA 19601
(C,S/pv,w)

Boro Industries, Inc.
P.O. Box 11558
Fort Worth, TX 76109
(C/pv,w)

Copco, Inc.
50 Enterprise Avenue
Secaucus, NJ 07094
(SP/p)

Coppes, Inc.
401 E. Market Street
Nappanee, IN 46550
(C/w)

Craft-Maid Custom Kitchens, Inc.
P.O. Box 4026
Reading, PA 19606
(C/pv,w)

Custom Furniture & Cabinets, Inc.
N. 55 Cedar Street
Post Falls, ID 83854
(C/pv,w)

Custom Wood Products, Inc.
P.O. Box 4516
Roanoke, VA 24015
(C/pv,w)

Diamond Cabinets
P.O. Box 547
Hillsboro, OR 97123
(S/w)

Elfa/West, Inc.
170 McCormick Avenue
Costa Mesa, CA 92626
(SP/m,i)

Grayline Housewares
1616 Berkeley Street
Elgin, IL 60120
(SP/m)

Haas Cabinet Co., Inc.
625 W. Utica Street
Sellersburg, IN 47172
(S/w)

Hager Manufacturing Co.
1522 N. Front Street
Box 1117
Mankato, MN 56001
(C/w)

Heidapal Designs, Inc.
719 Swift Street, No. 1
Santa Cruz, CA 95060
(C,SO/pv,w,i)

Hoffmeister Cabinets of Nevada
3069 Sheridan Street
Las Vegas, NV 89102
(C,S,SO/pv,w)

Home-Crest Corp.
P.O. Box 595
Goshen, IN 46526
(C,S/w)

Imperial Cabinet Co., Inc.
P.O. Box 427
Gaston, IN 47342
(SO/w)

Ingrid, Ltd.
3061 N. Skokie Highway
North Chicago, IL 60064
(SP/p)

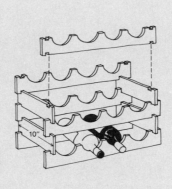
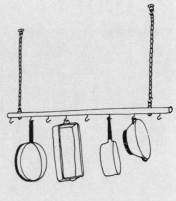

-Wood
P.O. Box 367
Milroy, PA 17063
(C/pv,w)

Capri Kitchens
P.O. Box 100
Dallastown, PA 17313
(C/w)

Kemper
01 South N Steet
Richmond, IN 47374
(S/pv,w)

Kent Moore Cabinets, Inc.
P.O. Box 3206
College Station, TX 77840
(C,SO/w)

Kitchen Kompact, Inc.
P.O. Box 868
Jeffersonville, IN 47130
(S/w)

Long Bell Cabinets
P.O. Box 579
Longview, WA 98632
(S/w)

Macor, Inc.
Cabinet Division
12 E. High Street
Mundelein, IL 60060
(C,S,SO/pv,w,i)

MasterCraft Industries Corp.
175 E. 39th Avenue
Denver, CO 80207
(S/pv,w)

Medallion Kitchens, Inc.
10 First Street South
Hopkins, MN 55343
(S,SO/w)

Merillat Industries, Inc.
075 W. Beecher Road
Adrian, MI 49221
(S/pv,w)

Merit Industries, Ltd.
12185 86th Avenue
Surrey, B.C.
Canada V3W-3H-8
(S/pv,w)

Micell Cabinet Corp.
501 Washington Avenue
Carlstadt, NJ 07072
(C/pv,w)

Overton Co.
P.O. Box 849
Kenly, NC 27542
(C,S,SO/pv,w)

Pacific Cabinet Corp.
Spokane Industrial Park
Building 26
Spokane, WA 99216
(C,S,SO/pv,w)

Pennville Custom Cabinets
P.O. Box 1266
Portland, IN 47371
(C/w)

Perfection Wood Products
7645 York Street
Denver, CO 80229
(C,SO/pv,w)

Plastics Unlimited, Inc.
Depot and First Streets
Youngwood, PA 15697
(C,S/pv)

Poggenpohl USA Corp.
P.O. Box 10
Teaneck, NJ 07666
(C/pv,w,i)

Prestige Cabinet Corp. of America
29 Rider Place
Freeport, NY 11520
(C/pv)

Prestige Products, Inc.
P.O. Box 314
Neodesha, KS 66757
(S/w)

Quaker Maid
Route 61
Leesport, PA 19533
(C,S/pv,w)

Quality Cabinets of Houston
6048 Westview
Houston, TX 77055
(C/w)

Rainier Woodworking Co.
16318 S. Meridian
Puyallup, WA 98371
(C/pv,w)

Rene Products
8600 Harrison Road
Cleves, OH 45002
(C,S/pv,w)

Rich Maid Kitchens, Inc.
Route 422
Wernersville, PA 19565
(C/w)

Rubbermaid Incorporated
1147 Akron Road
Wooster, OH 44691
(SP/p)

Rutt Custom Kitchens
Route 23
Goodville, PA 17528
(C/w)

Saint Charles Manufacturing Co., Inc.
1611 E. Main Street
Saint Charles, IL 60174
(C/pv,w)

Sawyer Cabinet, Inc.
12744 San Fernando Road
Sylmar, CA 91342
(C,S,SO/m,pv,w)

H. J. Scheirich Co.
P.O. Box 21037
Louisville, KY 40221
(S/w)

Schmidt-Haus
5237 Verona Road
Madison, WI 53711
(C,SO/pv)

Style-Line Manufacturing Co., Inc.
2081 S. 56th Street
West Allis, WI 53219
(C,S/pv,i)

Syroco
P.O. Box 4875
Syracuse, NY 13202
(SP/p)

Transco Plastics Corp.
26100 Richmond Road
Cleveland, OH 44146
(SP/p)

Triangle Pacific Corp.
P.O. Box 220100
Dallas, TX 75222
(C,S,SO/pv,w)

Waldorf Kitchens
Box 578
Waldorf, MD 20601
(C,S,SO/pv,w)

Wood Metal Industries
Wood Mode Cabinetry
Kreamer, PA 17833
(C/w)

XA Cabinet Corp.
16930 Valley View
La Mirada, CA 90638
(C,S/pv,w)

Yorktowne
P.O. Box 231
Red Lion, PA 17356
(S,SO/pv,w)

INDEX

PHOTOGRAPHERS

Glenn Christiansen: 10, 21 bottom. **Robert Cox:** 18, 71 bottom left and bottom right. **Jack McDowell:** 12 left and right, 13 left and right, 14 left and right, 15 top left, 16 right, 17 top and bottom, 20, 21 top, 22 left and right, 24 top, 33, 34, 36 left, 37 bottom, 38 top, 39 top, 40, 41 bottom, 43 top left and bottom right, 44, 45 left and right, 46 left and right, 47 right, 48 right, 57, 58 right, 60 bottom, 61 top left and bottom, 64 top and bottom, 65 top, 66, 68, 69 top left, 70 top, 71 top left. **Steve W. Marley:** 16 left, 19 left, 19 right, and bottom right, 24 bottom, 35 top right, 39 bottom middle, 41 top, 42, 43 top right, 47 left, 58 left, 59 top and bottom, 60 top, 62, 63 top left and bottom, 65 bottom left and bottom right, 69 right, 71 top right. **Don Normark:** 11 left, 72. **Rob Super:** 9 top and bottom, 11 right, 15 top right and bottom, 23 left and right, 35 bottom left, 36 right, 39 bottom right, 48 left, 63 top right, 67, 69 bottom left. **Darrow M. Watt:** 35 bottom right, 37 top, 61 right. **Tom Yee:** 38 bottom, 70 bottom.